TUMULT

TUMULT Botho Strauss
Botho Strauss TUMULT

Translated from the German by Michael Hulse

CARCANET PRESS MANCHESTER

First published in Great Britain 1984
by Carcanet Press Ltd
208 Corn Exchange Buildings, Manchester M4 3BQ
Translation © 1984 Michael Hulse
First published in 1980 by Carl Hanser Verlag,
*   titled* Rumor

The publisher acknowledges financial assistance
from the Arts Council of Great Britain

Strauss, Botho
   Tumult.
   I. Title   II. Rumor. *English*
   833'.914[F]   PT2681.T6869

   ISBN 0-85635-472-4

Typesetting by Paragon Photoset, Aylesbury
Printed in Great Britain by Short Run Press, Exeter

TUMULT

BEKKER really has come back.

Quite unexpectedly he has turned up at Zachler's monthly do. Bekker. Big sensation. Everyone crowds up to him, their man from outside who time and again found the courage to live without the Institute, or at least tried repeatedly to do so. But soon they move glumly away again, one after the other, just as in an advertisement a man with high hopes turns away from the woman with body odour and wrinkles his nose. Bekker barely says a word and silently assesses them all with looks accompanied, it seems, by a merciless remembering— his one-time colleagues and his host too, the boss, whose power goes on and on increasing.

Today he seems to me thinner than he was in former times, in spite of his height, in spite of his broad head with the hair combed smoothly back and the heavy bones of his forehead. His shoulders just sag. But that may be the fault of his comical, muddled clothing rather than a slipping of his bones. He is wearing a slack woollen cardigan with heart-shaped patches on the elbows, a colourful checked shirt underneath, and on his feet the clumsy kind of shoes, sturdy marching footwear, you get in *Bundeswehr* second-hand stores. Only his dark blue trousers with precise creases, wide in the leg and with deep turn-ups, are passable: a rather odd torso of evening elegance. His whole appearance in this uncoordinated, incompatible get-up has now an elderly, broken-down effect, now an effect of manly superiority. Bekker must in fact be in his early to mid-forties, indeed hardly older than myself. When his face is not moving, his eyes look mistily up from below, and his mouth is half open, he reminds one—sunken, burdened, spent—of an old man, or a man who has suddenly aged. On the other hand, as soon as he talks, and enjoys it, his

[1]

features grow tighter and his eyes keener. At first he does not notice me at all. Only when I finally cross over to him and embrace him does he thaw; he feels more comfortable and comes out of himself a little. He mentions Oldenburg and his troubles there during the last two years only briefly. It is behind him and has been of little profit. The immediate effect of this reunion, the charisma of his personality, his flaring intelligence, cast a spell on me immediately. I can listen to him only vaguely and with my concentration failing. I just think: with all the effete posing of the rest of us, Bekker's manner is truly incisive. If ever he had power (and wanted to have it!) he could attract more people, and bind them closer to him, than Zachler even, who has reached the stage of seducing and shining by virtue of his position alone, and in himself has hardly a spark left. That aside, it makes me rather nervous that Bekker no longer calls me simply Bruno as he used to but constantly Bruno Stöss; that is to say, calls me by my whole name, a cool or semi-confiding address such as officers of equal rank or celebrities sometimes use to each other.

Bekker and I began together in Zachler's Institute, twelve years ago. It goes by the somewhat high-flown name of Institute, the Institute for News and Information, the INI, and in reality is no more than a quite ordinary firm of medium size, that deals in information, trend reports and model plans rather than ball-bearings or sporting equipment; a private, limited liability enterprise, with an owner and some three dozen employees, all of whom—with the exception of the office and book-keeping personnel—are specialists in particular technical or scientific fields. The Institute peddles know-how in practically every important area of activity in modern society. Here we all work under the same roof: manager, adminis-trative lawyer, information scientist, urban developer, but also experts on tourism, psychology, and social pedagogics. Everyone is responsible for keeping abreast of the latest developments in his field, analyses news, prepares background reports which are sent in the form of so-called newsletters to our subscribers: clients in economics, teaching,

[2]

and political organizations. Although all that is involved is ready-to-use knowledge, which we adeptly arrange and market, and although the idea content of the product we sell for good money does not originate in our own creative endeavour, now and then Zachler does not hesitate to call his Institute 'a small university in its own right', and to deck out himself and his colleagues with exalted labels of intellectual value.

I very well understand that Bekker has always detested our business, the entire way in which Zachler runs it and personifies the power of the blueprint, the way we others (and I admit it: all of us) do no more than circle about Zachler and identify totally with him as soon as we are called on to act as leaders ourselves. Someone like Bekker must always have found this repellent. Still, you have to take into consideration that he himself failed by a long way to forge that career in the Institute that would bind a man on his way to the top more and more intimately to the business, finally in every fibre of his being. He had come to Zachler as a young man who had given up his law studies and right away had contributed an abundance of fruitful ideas to the expansion of the Institute; for a while he was even reckoned to be the boss's most intimate associate, without actually having precisely defined duties of his own. Then in later years, when the multiplicity of departments increased and a nicely meticulous consensus had often to be worked out among the experts, you saw how the ground gradually slipped away from under his feet, how he busied himself patiently and knowledgeably about too much and nothing, how gradually he was left behind and became insignificant in the firm. After all, he had never headed a department singly, indeed, had merely superintended a group project. Instead, he ran away repeatedly. I believe he tried three or four times to put the Institute behind him and to regain a foothold at the university. He would be offered participation in a research programme or a commissioned study, in Dortmund or Oldenburg or somewhere. And there were interim periods too, in which he was more or less twiddling his thumbs. At times he was obliged to muddle along as a product tester or salesman, an interviewer or taxi-driver. So now it looks as if he's standing at the gates once again.

The Institute is a shit-house of the spirit and a breeding-ground of idiocy. You resemble that point of light with a flickering tail, a flagellate, that always follows the same path on an oscillograph, vanishes, appears again on the other side of the screen, again follows the same path, and with a differential of ± 2mm measures the precision of the welding of systems. To be that point and nothing else. It is only the drill and the false world-view of the fakir's way of life that have taught us to put up with such consumption and such stabbing-pains in the heart. The longer I stare at the screen the more clearly I see the various stages of man's development into an idiot pass before my eyes. I see them presented by a totally everyday example of the species, most probably I myself, who ceaselessly walks along the high wall that surrounds the Institute, at times runs away, at times creeps, squats and craps, scratches at the wall and listens for answering scratches, leans and clings by suction to the thick stonework, tries to embrace the wall with wide-open arms, leaps at it like a dog, and then once again just walks, walks, walks. . . . I must needs think incessantly of reason, like an idiot who has long since lost it and dully ponders it. When it comes to it we are all idiots, mentally retarded, with a deep submissiveness. Obedience and blind slavery to those natures whose ego is strong, imitation of your superior, addiction, the passion to submit to attachment at any price, even if it means giving up yourself: this disease is now spreading among us to a horrifying extent. One of our most capable news analysts, Krähkamp, has by now transformed himself completely into a copy of the boss. It extends into your vocabulary and intonation, your choice of clothing and cigarette, and even the bad habit of finishing a man's sentence for him before he's finished speaking has been taken over from

Zachler, from the boss. In this way it goes the rounds. Those who lack a powerful self, among them educated, cultivated men as well as coarse louts and clueless innocents, totter half-smothered along our corridors and regain their poise and breath only when they are allowed to plunge into the bracing ether of some ego-hero. But outside the firm, among friends and acquaintances, things are also much the same: everyone hunts for a leader in his immediate neighbourhood, his guru, his life-giver, be it the boss or a doctor or an aikido master. In every corner some commander of mankind arises, a charismatic little shaman. And they of course succeed in setting free the so-called unsuspected latent powers of their vassals, and once set free, as a rule these powers leave behind a totally emptied vessel. The strong egos grow stronger day by day. To those they are allowed to follow, verminous geniuses, voracious wrecks, they attribute one greatness after the other, since after all nobody cares to be the servant of an insecure weakling. Me, needless to say, Mr Average that I am, they carefully leave aside. No one can get the ray treatment he needs under my myopic pupils. When I talk, people tend to think of something else. . . . Oh yes, go ahead, see through the whole ridiculous show, how your friends get tangled and all the others too. Yet seeing through it is so entirely useless! As long as you yourself are not involved anywhere and perpetually stand coldly aside, it is easy to see through it all, and still you long for the tiniest teardrop of devotion, enough to bring a hint of dimness into the eye.

Something's up. People are behaving more and more peculiarly. In the midst of the party Martin lies down on the couch in the next room, in Zachler's library, and writhes in anguish, complains that Joe isn't paying him back the thirty-eight Swiss francs he's owed him since last Easter without being reminded. He wails at finding himself so little thought of, at realizing no one remembers such trivialities where he's concerned. I'd say he's exaggerating. So is the Flensch woman. Suddenly she screams like a stuck pig, out in the hall, just because her woman-friend left the street door open after saying goodbye and walking out to her car. What's the matter? A girl I don't know, perhaps from the mailing department: suddenly out of the blue, as if a volcano had spat it out, she emits a fiery torrent of spite across the bent back of her cavalier, whose every word, a moment before, she was absorbing with such rapt addiction. I was just thinking: how she can listen!—and she bats her eyelids at this costly part of his face, his lips, restless, an inscrutable treasure—I thought: they're warming up truly shamelessly, here among all the people they're warming up for bed, and just a moment before she's all ears while her friend jokes with the host, she hangs on his every little quip, always the first to giggle hectically; and then, after they have bent over the table and whispered to each other, suddenly she stands bolt upright, trembling, her whole face chalk-white, her mouth hissing rabidly down at him, and tears her dress in half from top to bottom before him and empties the heaped-full ashtray over her hair, and runs out clamouring and doubled up, kicking her shoes, her steep cork buskins, off her feet, runs barefoot with the flapping flag of her torn dress through the crowded company out into the street. . . . What word had been spoken, which alone was so powerful as to call forth from this young little larva, from the midst of a splendid togetherness, from one moment to the next, a rage—and farewell—of such primaeval power?

Highly affronted natures, rocking to and fro on the tiptoes of their being. Many who have no idea at all about what is going on, and suddenly they moan as if they were being tortured, cry out as if someone had set fire to them, all on account of a draught! Or gasping into the nothing of an underground train they've missed as if it was the face of the Gorgon. These people often seem no longer capable of performing the simplest functions of their species and at the slightest mishap they lament like ancient warriors threatened by the gods. They exaggerate. They seek to wear themselves out at all costs. With the finest style they capitulate at the slightest provocation. They exaggerate and no longer fit their normal shell and are incapable, as they grow older in their little

[6]

shell, of gliding to and fro in a moderate way. They are thrown by the way their lives are.

A little later Grit, Bekker's daughter, appears at the party too. I have not seen her for some years and am astonished to see what a self-confident, beautiful young woman she has turned into. She is in a bad mood and sulks. At first she has only two things to say—that is, that she could find nowhere for miles around to park but a pavement space three streets beyond the water-works, and then in the same breath that she's just going through a separation, it's dreadful. She says it in a throwaway manner, as other people let you know that they've recently given up smoking or have gone on a diet. It soon becomes apparent that father and daughter stand together somewhat uncertainly, indeed, almost embarrassed, and attempt to close themselves off from the rest of the guests. You can tell by looking at them that they've only recently seen each other and have noticed considerable changes. All those years after the divorce, when Grit was living with her mother, during her schooldays and her training as a foreign language secretary, her father's visits remained few and far between and almost always went off dismally, with the bickering demands that the separated parents made of each other. It seemed as if Bekker never knew a particularly heartfelt closeness to his daughter. He only rarely spoke of her. Now, once again on the return to Zachler's Institute, he seeks her out in the city—by now she is living in a flat of her own and has leased a small travel agency, since she has not been able to fulfil her wish to find a good position abroad—and so all of a sudden he encounters a grown-up, independent person in whom his own child seems partly to have vanished and partly to be within reach at last for the first time. Grit too does not behave as if her father had never been away. Both of them appraise each other with extreme caution and with glances that are at times insecure and strange, and this takes on an odd artificiality and tenseness in view of their blood relationship and conspicuous facial

[7]

resemblance. Presently the crowd and the noise in the room bother them and they move into an adjoining room, Zachler's wife's studio, which has been meticulously stripped of all personal belongings, and there they find the quiet necessary to ask questions softly and to speak with ever greater freedom. Grit tells the latest about her mother, who lives in southern Germany with an estate agent, talks of Joseph, her friend, from whom she is just separating, about music that they both liked listening to and other music that they quarrelled over. Most of it comes superficially, very little from within. Bekker, on the other hand, bares his breast, as you might say, once he is sure that Grit is not out to revive memories and his past as a bad father is not up for discussion. He feels an urge to confide in her mother and more boldly, exactly as if the burden of silence before the child of immature understanding, which for over two decades she has been for him, were finally falling from him with a thump. He talks agitatedly, and frequently in dark, abrupt fantasies that betray little concerning his doings and activities, his outer life, but a good deal of his condition, his restless spirit that kicks in every direction at once. They sit next to each other on two straight-backed chairs designed by the hostess herself, and Bekker gulps agitatedly from the bottle of cognac that Zachler pushed into his grasp as a gesture of special humiliation, a mute, intimate welcome. The more he drinks, the more exquisitely and animatedly Grit is present, listening, wonderfully listening, the more recklessly does her father hold forth about his fragmented world, and there is no sign of his speech ending: it bears them both into the small hours, when forks rattle in the kitchen for a herring snack, and again and again he takes his daughter's hand and holds it tight over his knee. Now and then guests leaving to go home pause in the open door, some even come in, listen for a short while and then disappear again. Shortly before the pick-me-up break-fast the children are already up and about, delighting in the deso-late, dirty house. In their eyes Bekker too is part of the debris of the party's aftermath. They romp about him and climb up him and, sliding off his shoulders, call him a drunken mountain.

[8]

I GREW UP under the heavy winter-campaign trench-coat of a wrathful officer who was not my father but who, in his place, took terrible care of my mother and me—a major in Hitler's *Ostarmee*, prematurely returned home from the forests of Kalinin, dishonourably discharged, accused of insubordination, a toppled, tattered warrior hungry for revenge, high-handed, tenderly disposed to me alone, his beloved protégé, and filling me with the concentrated remainder of the energies inspiriting his life: hatred, contempt, the urge to destroy, and a death-wish. . . . Thus this shadow again rises mightily behind my back and it is as if that early evil were only now properly taking effect and were making the cramped circumference of the steps I take in life contract ever smaller, presently, perhaps, to end in a crazy whirlwind around its own axis. I stand once again—doubtless for the last time—before the Institute entrance, to which as a young man, escaping from my oppressive background, I fled as to a temple of bliss, and where, I told myself, I should at last attain a free development, good and correct instruction, meaning in my life; and where I then, under Zachler's rule, landed in the most terrible prison that a human being hoping for independence can land in. Four times—all in all, four times in my life—I have tried to escape from this magic prison and find work and a living elsewhere. Again and again I have been drawn back, in a nauseating but irresistible way; again and again, and every time unhappier, I have returned.

Zachler's Institute, the INI, where only mediocre people or failures, who could be paid a fairly low salary, worked, or, as in my case (a beginner who had broken off his studies), next to nothing; an apprentice, who, as soon as he had been brought by the firm's bus at half-past seven along with secretaries and accountants, had to do simply everything, from emptying wastepaper baskets to drafting advertisements, and who, in the process, got so much wrong that he was frequently given to considering, with affected concern, what a hard time he would have outside the firm, how hard, or even impossible, it would undoubtedly be to get by outside in what was generally a far tougher professional life. In this way at every rank and level Zachler's people were and are kept dependent. They are kept artificially in their mediocrity or failure, so that, with their low salaries, which remain low, fearfully they cling to the whole family in the firm: Zachler and the departmental heads. Naturally there were occasionally others, apart from myself, who left the firm on their own initiative and looked for something better outside. And naturally the attempt always ended in failure, since the firm had, after all, been the breeding-ground of their complexes and weaknesses for long enough. But then, what a red-letter day for the board, what a powerful confirmation of the family!—when one of these unfortunates quietly came asking if there was a chance of being reappointed. The board, Zachler himself, greeted and embraced each one of these climbers *manqués* with the greatest heartiness and shoved him into his old place of work or even into one a grade lower. Nearly always the home-comer then felt far, far better in his old family than he had before his attempt to escape. Generally the board was able to rely on him for good from then on.

As far as I know I am the only one who has tried it more than once. If I am employed again—and it will assuredly be the last time—an ominous post somewhere in the Monitoring Department threatens, the most reviled section of the entire firm; it has already become the catch-phrase most readily used for warning blundering analysts—'I shouldn't send this in unless you want to end up in Monitoring.'

So now, on the rebound to Zachler, the major-monster rises again at my back, the dreadful educator. Now this figure again forces himself into the foreground, a stone-drunk, heavy man whom I had to shake so often when he clawed into the soil and tulips in the spa park or, as once happened, fell into a display window on the way home. In those days, back home, down by the Lahn. All these years I've not given him another thought, this domestic fool with the face of a Silenus, the clamorous enemy of the state pensioned off, boiling up revenge on his wretched commander fresh each day with his breakfast milk; but then, half way, his head gave way after all. Robbed of his enemy, of fighting, of killing, he circled lifelessly about, only offering up a sleepy repetition of the old hatred, his great condemnations that at one time made up the entire heat of his person. A father and a slaughterer, dishonourably discharged, now he approaches once again, drapes his heavy coat across my shoulders so that I will draw myself up to full stretch just like the unrecognizable man with the umbrella and bloody mouth under the cadaver of beef in Francis Bacon's painting. Let yourself go once more, have a fling, right? And then in perfect silence withdraw to the Institute . . .

So let us walk about the city. Let's look around. We have arrived. Here it is, Tartary. There's no more to come. From far, far under the earth, where the ancients supposed it to be, our underworld has surged up high unto daylight, a hell that anyone can walk in. . . . Stay with me. Talk to me. The drunk is carried home by the early morning rays. . . . No, this is not a sign of things to come: there's nothing more. We have arrived. Let us look around. Don't let's wait any longer. Let us look around in this dirty little, beastly, cramped, slovenly damnation. . . . Here in this sealed–up house you will find a quite ordinary concentration camp, one among millions. A man is mistreating his wife. You hear the naked limbs with their depressions slap against the tiled bathroom wall. He shakes her by the shoulders as you might try to shake more sound out of an ancient portable radio. He throws her about the room, her bones, muffled by skin and flesh, bash against

[11]

the tiles. See, he hits her, but she doesn't fall down. She doesn't fall, and she is silent. She holds herself upright against the wall, her back to him. Slowly she draws away from him, along the tiles, to get to the wash-basin. He tears her round by the shoulder and smashes his fist into her face. She totters but does not fall. She looks at him and once again stands erect, turned toward him. A brown contusion swells, darkening her eye as a sepia cloud obscures the menaced octopus. Watery snot runs from her nostrils. Now she turns round again since she wants to get to the wash-basin. With her naked back before him he swings both clenched hands far back over his head, as if he were holding an axe, and brings his hands down so that they hit the sensitive lump of her cervical vertebra. The woman stretches her arms half-up by way of reflex, as one of those lead table footballers in the old days would propel its leg forward when you turned it on its head, and spreads all her fingers out so stiffly that her ring springs to the floor from her ring finger. Then she falls, hits her forehead and forearm against the edge of the bath before her lean body bangs angularly on to the floor tiling, falling badly. In falling she has caught up a bar of soap from the edge of the bath; it slithers across the tiles. The woman, see, lifts herself up again immediately, she does not let herself go, and grabs the bar of soap and places it dazedly back in its place. She tries to stand up, but falls over on to the floor again. Suddenly a small quantity of bright, almost white urine is emitted from her body. She looks at it and, inter-rupted in what is actually her fate, looks up at her husband, inconsolably amazed, and tears gather in her eyes. Her husband grabs her head and pushes it down. He wipes up the puddle on the tiles with her hair. Thus it continues and will never end, the half-dressed man, the naked woman. Kill each other? Talk about it? Unnecessary. A short while later, as soon as he touches her forehead gently once more, merely at the touch of his hand this woman, from out of her tortured contortions, already begins the even, worm-like movements of surrender. She whips her pelvis up and down, gasps, responds to the touch of his hands, her eyes open wide and a

[12]

little vein bursts, her white eyeball becomes bloody and she tears at her own hair and slobbers. Now she is at her climax, a climax of self, and would eat anything that was crammed into her mouth, for she wants to be and at the same time to devour everything that human life can give in one go: man and woman, child and ancient, power and punishment, shit and breath, exalted and debased, believing and blaspheming, murderer and victim—everything paired, everything at once, in one single momentary bloody round-dance . . .

She is, by the by, the same woman who laughed out loud that morning when the boss gave her husband a dressing-down before her eyes, annihilated him and made him an object of ridicule. She joined in the laughter then on the side of the boss, who persisted in addressing her husband as 'champ', and in her eyes too, which belonged to her boss, her lord and master was suddenly the champion duffer. She laughed and was still smiling long after the boss had finished joking and was killing with looks.

But the day will come too when she squats alone down there, alone in this place of the dead, this tiled wilderness, and then we shall see her raving, scratching with her finger-nails at the sealed-up earth. But this is Tartary. Here neither grave nor nourishment can be dug up. You cannot go deeper than the tiled-up earth.

Silent torture and extermination chamber. The bed a blood-filled pit. The camp in everyone. Arena without sound. Unswerving, hither and thither through the insurgent part of town a woman drives in a loudspeaker van like those political parties use for campaign announcements, and pages her husband: Philipp! and his passport photo, as large as a political poster, practically dissolving into unrecognizability in the enlargement, is on the vehicle's roof, fastened to the loud-speaker. She says that she forgives him unconditionally and he should return to her. She asks the population to look for him and send him to her.

But be careful, Philipp! Do not trust this vehicle, from which the voice of your beloved sounds in the streets below. She has gone over to the rulers, or rather they have black-mailed her, taken her hostage, to lure you into a trap. Do not go down, resist these painful calls of reconciliation, even if it seems to you that her love has never sounded more intense than through this wretched wandering loudspeaker. She will betray you—must betray you—and tomorrow they will drag you into the stadium, where meanwhile over twenty thousand people have been penned up, watched over and kept in order by hundreds of military myrmidons. All families torn apart, the old people are compelled to clean the arena in blistering heat, till they fall down to left and right of the ash tracks. The men are ordered away to put on fights, east block against north, just as it comes. The women and children have to sew all superfluous clothing into gigantic sun-protection awnings, and in every block there is one of those who were shot while trying to escape, fastened head down to a mast, visible far and wide by way of deterrent. This one who was hanged has had his tongue pulled far out and pierced with a thick needle. From this needle hangs the phrase for the day, written on a little scrap of paper, and every one of the prisoners' spokesmen has to go up close to the tongue early each morning to read the meaningless wisdoms that the dictatorship has inscribed in its tiny, decorative hand: 'Little-lonely-skeleton. That is man's career'. Similar demoralizing sayings are then proclaimed all day long.

God knows nothing of all this. He does not know what has become of us. All that remains of Him is a little table under the naked, glaring light of a bulb that hangs from an invisible ceiling, and a chair tipped over backwards that this prison warder has abandoned in leaping to his feet to pace the Great Official Wall of the establishment; a moment ago I saw so much of Him, when in the frigid silence his fountain pen rolled off the table and broke on the tiles. He made a blot, this warder, he left us a dark blot. Once before I had to grope for foreign words about the camps in godforsaken drunkenness: it

[14]

was abroad, probably 44th Street in New York, the bar for asexuals, to which one of Zachler's secretaries had dragged me since at that time it was brand new and you just had to have seen it—men and women who somehow had it behind them and were sociably relaxing from each other. It was already a favourite meeting-place and the room was full to bursting. I remember that I told the girl of the biologists' experiment: cramming field-mice cruelly together and then, after a while, watching how at first the little creatures' fur stood on end and they arched their backs, then the males lost the urge and the ability to copulate, and finally cannibalism became wide-spread. . . . We were standing immediately behind the row of bar stools, constantly being shoved to and fro and often so far apart that I almost had to shout when I was talking. In German. After a while someone next to me slides down from his stool, a man of about sixty, bows to my face and declares he can't stand German at his back, hearing German spoken here in the bar, not at any price this evening. I stop him—in English—and ask him to sit down again. When I speak English he unbends, his choler is somewhat allayed. He murmurs that he really can't forget, and as it were by the way, with a shrug of his shoulders, as he pushes his backside on to the stool again, he tells me the reason, and the reason is of course the camps, the German ones. I still remember how I was shocked, with a sense of shame and defiance, to find that someone had leapt from his seat and had been within an ace of hitting me in the gob simply because I was speaking my mother tongue. I believe I then sat on into the early hours of the morning with this lonely, tormented drinker, and we ordered one Canadian whisky after another. He could no longer get off the subject of the camps at all, and to every appalling fact that he presented, slamming it down on the counter with the flat back of his hand, he added this mulishly accusing 'Why?' as if I were supposed to make up on the spot for what was owed. A family wiped out—why? Without permitting even a hint of an answer, or of a more thorough questioning, he was only interested in totting up a longer and more terrible list, and I, in

[15]

order to prove my sympathy, could find nothing better to do than in the end simply to bid as well and, in a veritable *danse macabre* poker, to play the atrocities I knew of for what they were worth. At times it seemed to me that he was seeking out and savouring in this subject a dull, malicious thrill, the greatness of a righteous shudder, which the foul, hollowed-out life of recent years could offer nothing to compare with. At the end, at any rate, we were speaking thick and we circled babbling about the unspeakable camp, which, the drunker we became, raised its serpent's head all the more mightily and I, groping for words, constantly in fear lest the slightest little word of German slip out inadvertently, was already ashamed of my coarse German accent and was all the time afraid that this mere undertone of German in everything I uttered would suddenly transport him into a rage again . . .

No, and on the other hand I was not ashamed. To tell the truth, I felt something of a refractory pride in being a German, precisely because here you had to earn that status, because it required a certain effort and you didn't cash in your welcome for free. I also—I can't say why—suddenly felt a tremendous stab of homesickness and love of my country. Rather: of a no doubt imaginary country.

That German had not been destroyed in this unique machinery for extermination, that Hitler had not succeeded in cremating the German language too (and that only genuine Swiss today possessed the German language!)—this whole business of being German in spite of Hitler gave me pleasure deep down, while up above I stammered and stuttered in English; nor did I feel ashamed that it was the camp that we were stammering and stuttering about—in the end I even found it worthy of the inexpressible that we kept on repeating in a heavy humourless stupor the same comment on the subject: why?

These people in quest of quiet have laid down their arms before elusive Sexus, then. There they sit, crowded together,

[16]

and don't want to play any more. Sexus, the adventuring spirit of disappointment, which leads to crime, murder, self-destruction, is not worth the wager any more. The focal point of everything we have ever developed as the sense of promises and the power to fail is in fact slipping out of focus. Desire, which never was naked, which always pursued many ends in many veils but aimed to rip these veils to shreds and play a hermetic game, has bit by bit stripped itself of vice and sin, of love and domestic convenience. They live more comfortably alone, none are protected by families any more, and they have even put an end to longing.

That time on 44th Street—I had no notion! I had no notion of that man who is remembering today. And this unknowing yesterday, an animal innocence never experienced, this creature now chases you through the streets. You resemble the actor learning his lines, running shouting across the fields, pursued by countless ghosts, desert snakes, creditors, all the avenging spirits of the soul; the actor who hastens along the theatre's corridors, tosses his coat to the house manager and plunges on to the stage, into the bright, concealing cone of light—who closes the heavy wing portal of the set behind him, shoots the bolt, puts his weight against it, piles a cupboard, a chair, a triumphal column, and anything else he can remove from the set against the door, against which spirits pound and push from outside—who slides to the floor on the stage, exhales profoundly, the audience in front of him: saved. A moment ago still a place of refuge, the stage is then transformed into a place of horror. In the back wall of the closed, heavy back-drop a far bigger door opens than the one the actor has just barricaded, a high oak portal in the panelling of which the barricaded door is no more than one lower postern serving as entrance and exit for the small and weak; and the hand of a colossus, a gigantic hand clad in a dark, unbuttoned leather glove, reaches through the gap and in the cupped palm of this hand a little heap of human beings scramble about; and a terrible wind pours through this opening too, the hand shakes its occupants off, and they tumble from some height down to

[17]

the stage floor, the portal creaks shut, all but a minute crevice from which air continues to hiss on to the stage. Those who have been thrown out run around panic-stricken, yelling. But the one who just exhaled so profoundly on the stage is snatched up by the wind and flung among those who are milling about, who are all yelling nothing but names, like survivors of a shipwreck calling for their dearest ones, and indeed among them he finds one who clings to him and only to him; they embrace in the violent storm right next to the crack and exchange a few promises. . . . Then, as always happens in the theatre, it suddenly goes dark and silent. It has been nothing. The people can go home. They have seen two people hugging and struggling against the gale. The woman was yelling into the wind. The man—with the wind—was able to whisper. Then a sudden whirlwind separated the two, swept them into the air like leaves and tore them apart, last of all their hands. Unforgettable: her hand and his stretched out, and all that remains to be considered is this image of a rift in which it will later be impossible to tell whether the hands are approaching or parting from each other. Reaching out or turning away? Farewell, or a beginning? You can't tell, but you can't forget it.

Let us walk the city, a little further into the petrified forest full of frozen transformation, multiplying division. A little more walking, catabasis, not too fast. . . . Head held up for sound and shadow alone. (Whatever you whistle this morning is a Fascist melody, a hangman's tremolo, and looking at your watch on your wrist is Fascist too—indeed, your wrist itself *is* brutal, is Fascist . . . everything that occurs to you this morning has been concocted by evil and pitilessness. The arseless are inferior.) But how on earth do we get these couples coming so strangely together everywhere, in corners and in pools of sunshine? Loving each other, satisfying, the kiss as food or as . . . what-you-may-call-it, oh, a good intention, the old story. But those? They have had their visages sealed for ever by mistrust and grinning. None can smile. Why then root about in the mouths of strangers?

[18]

There is someone in a lightless light-shaft.

The officer who is getting dressed, presumably strapping on his braces, dressing rather ceremoniously and, as it turns out, in consequence of the lack of light, totally untidily. Likewise his wife there in the far corner in front of a mirror without light. And now that light does in fact drift in she snaps round, shocked and malicious, toward it, fighting it, shooing it, shows it her backside, makes obscene noises in her mouth and holds the mirror up to the light.

She runs to the end of the corner. There she is found.

A fear is abroad in the land, as if the Duke of Württemberg were once again enlisting young men to present to England as soldiers. . . . Smash the whole tendency. Create shadows and Every day is like that in the guts. Many days, after Oldenburg. Why are they shooting? . . .

God, he had to be led to the telephone in the end, by force. He really thought it was an animal! His fear had to be taken from him, he had to be led there and shown how it's done, picking up the receiver in your hand . . . in your hand! Like this, damn it! Don't throw it down! Hold on to it! . . . This is where you speak and this is where you listen. . . . Right! Do it! . . . Well, in the end he did speak to her. That was the officer. Completely thrown after the death of Hanni, his first wife, lifted out of the light-shaft, the old man, and now he means to orient himself in all his wanderings through the city, always and everywhere, with his sense of history. 'We were so far from the centre there, in our little corner we could repeat and repeat great things endlessly, ape all the significant alliances in world history in our little corner, and far away from everything act big. . . .' Can you perhaps let me know just once how, at these hurricane-like volumes, with this punk, you still mean to orient yourself with your ear and your sense of history? The youngest are just listening to Nazi shockers on record. Children's memories are in any case meddled with. The tissue is destroyed. School first. Instead of the history and deciphering of cultures they learn to watch television rationally. School! Hand in hand with the daily

[19]

extinguishing job done by television, this thick, white extinguishing foam which smothers whatever fire of craving or woe there might be in the children. I tell you: one or two generations more and people wholly free of memory will be drifting through their fates. They will simply have forgotten everything. After us they will forget everything. After us they will forget everything that once was. . . . All this blether of history. Was something there? . . . The people at the Institute say you should already consider the matter rather as a kind of wide-area relay. Not root, depth or origin any more but the relay, countless circuits at one time on one level, humming away, connections and enormous accumulations in storage, a chip, a minute control particle, electronic superbrains, you can readily dispense with five thousand manual workers, big as the tip of your thumb, a chip; nothing deep-going, not depth, but the small, flat desolate relays . . . ('Do you know anything about this?' the boss asks at the other end of the line, so that the receiver swims in the sweat of your hand . . .) Liberation from the nineteenth century! . . . we demand . . . now, at the end of the twentieth, at long last . . . with a great, once-only, positively final rearing-up (of the cadaver, weighed down by the billions of termites feeding on it) into the next epoch, borne to fresh pastures of perception, where finally the order of the day is to think everything that we have collected, to stretch on one spot and distribute round about all we have already got together in the way of property, spirit, history. Probably there has long been enough. Probably we now have more or less everything at our disposal and no more will be added to it.

But the point is: hanging on to the globe with such un-differentiated thoughts I sit in the bus early in the morning and someone I don't know behind me, who cannot control his joy at a prospective promotion or his joy in existence itself, hits me (me!) on the head with his rolled-up morning paper. Just like that—because he feels good, too good! I cannot contain myself with humiliation. I do not even look up and stare at him—I could not do so with tears in my eyes. Now he whistles to boot. And melodiously too! I do not dare move and press my hands between my knees. At most you do things like that among friends, I think, and even there it is an annihilating smack! So I have already reached the point where a stranger can drum on my head with a rolled-up newspaper. Yes, I am already at that point, and a good deal further, when later in a choking midday dream my mother looks at me across the fruit-press in the kitchen where in past days I often sat with her and hoarded up this or that slight of the morning inside me— even my own mother's recommendation today is . . . after I have spent long enough dismissing every one of her honest consolations, moodily, even frostily, intending to demand of her on each occasion a profounder, even better thought-out consolation, forcing her to exert the fantasy of her heart to the uttermost for once, till at last I have driven her to a well-nigh speechless, pitying groaning from which, since I am more and more recklessly and shockingly miserable and reproach her with myself, her goodness at last produces this final pro- nouncement . . . 'How on earth do you intend to get through a long, long life if you torment yourself so?' . . . Ah, indeed, suicide! This is her entire apothecary, at least to consider doing away with oneself, eh? 'But,' she cries, pleading, as I now laugh with the bitterest contentment, 'but how, how?' . . . In the womb it is just as clammy as everywhere else in the underworld. Who is surprised by this? The breed of angels has shot up high under the toxic dust, has coarsened to colossal dimensions. If now one were to lead you, the least touch of his wing would knock you to the ground. His face is a round, weathered millstone. Clumsily the guardian monster reels and falls from the sky right above you. . . . How am I, a warrior torn in half, to rise from Frau Zachler's home-made furniture? The drunk is borne home by the rays of morning. Maybe. I shall roam on slowly, through the town, Grit, as there is a tumult down there which I must hear. . . . A bell swings its alarm at the top of the belfry, but it is empty and without its

[21]

clapper sends no sound across the land apart from a cutting hissing of air. The platinum blonde whore sits on one of the palm-tubs with which the city council, in a surprise move, has afforested her beat. There she sits in her saffron-yellow pants on the fresh earth of the tub and pulls her stockings straight, all set for resistance. I won't be thrust away into the jungle here on my very own platform, she thinks. She contemplates the new back-drop like an opera star guesting in a different production. So she sits for a while, stupidly absorbed, as slack and lost in thought as if she were in her own kitchen, on the edge of the tub, only to make her entrance suddenly after all, erect and bent out straight, in her pointed shoes. And yet she has forgotten to shake herself down! Black earth clings to the seat of her yellow pants and only a little crumbles away. Such a forgotten spot on someone who advertises with a flawless figure attracts attention, and those who pass grin immediately, but no one says anything to her, she who is so ostentatious with her behind! The goods ought to be clean. But I am attracted by precisely that: the way she notices nothing and walks so lightly and evenly that she can still round and point her finger-nails with the finest of files as she walks. I'll take her.

In the hotel, under the roof, where a one-time loft has been divided into tiny cabins with plywood walls, a couple in the next room who are melancholy and fettered with dismal worries ruin our enthusiasm. The woman, shaken by intense pauses, repeatedly stammers out the same words of love. A German, half-swallowed sound. For the man there is constantly something that he calls a frightful problem, in a hollow, mulish monotone, a frightful problem, while she, in counterpoint, continues her unvarying aria: 'It's so beautiful with you . . . you're so loving . . . you love me so well . . . I love you so much . . . what's up with you? . . . what do you want? . . . Come here . . . Give me your hand. . . . Tell me what you want. . . . Yes.' But the man remains lost in thought and doesn't budge on his bed. They are travelling, have gone on a trip, he is with his lover, and his wife, on the brink of putting an end to it all, has remained at home, and

[22]

now he phones her several times a day from service areas and post offices, thinking he has to, to keep her from the worst. Recently she has answered mildly and absently at the receiver, has asked for forgiveness, gives confused answers, as if an overdose were already bearing her inexorably away from everything worldly. In this way she gives him a bad conscience, her last and most certain means of putting him off his trip and his bed, though also off returning at all. And beyond the thin wall the man suddenly exclaims: 'If she killed herself it would really be the best thing for her!' . . . Well, my little platinum blonde whore, that was no pious wish. But it's not infrequently that you hear things like that. Those who are inhuman through passion under pressure, the bed intimate, the life of those who are sick with love and those who are not loved any more not worth living. 'Let your soul take a good deep breath,' says his woman–friend next door, as expected, stupidly and moved; and, agreeably horrified from top to toe, she again cuddles up to him. The familiar seductive whispers start up anew and the unchangeable curving lines that her hand has already travelled over so many different bodies and which nonetheless always remain the same. 'I love you so much . . . you're so loving . . . you love me so well. . .'. Oh, my little whore, I tell you: the way people talk in this endless samey humdrum is exactly the way they feel, and not a jot more. The entire life of the soul revolves in a sluggish whirlpool of repetitions and we do not have more than a handful of more profound emotions. For we have all of us been cast with a single throw of the dice . . .

Look, that one comes from the East. Her generous friend has improved everything about her, her clothing is fresh and Western from tip to toe, a French neckerchief, blouse, waistcoat, but her shoes Italian. All they forgot was her spectacles. The frame is still Eastern. Her spectacles clearly give away where she comes from. She has solemnly entered into her first great bondage, following a man over the border whom she got to know when he was engaged in cathedral studies in Magdeburg. After one and a half years of a satisfied *relationship* the first moments when they recognize each other are creeping in. But while she only loves him all the more maturely after every emptiness she rides out, the painter is soon no longer able to conceal that he is tired of her, irreversibly, just as in this country people sooner or later grow tired of shoes, scarves or spectacle frames for no pressing reason. You always find something better. And you poke about listlessly in the most wonderful dishes, listlessly in the loveliest hips.

For a whole night she whom he no longer wishes to see stands down in the street and calls his name up to the window. Up in his studio he does not move: whatever you do, don't cast a shadow. The front door remains locked. She lies across the bonnet of his white Citroën. Cries and dozes. Every now and then she wakes and brings her hand down thunderously on the metal of the bonnet. No! No! No! she bawls. Then she slumps forward again, cries and dozes.

How have I come by such infernal power, the painter wonders up above, that another human being can abase herself before me in this way? He sits despondently in his big, bare factory floor, his studio. The windows are still half open, so that her noise and cries can enter. A gentle breeze wafts morning across. The presenter of the radio programme 'Music till morning' has long since gone home and his colleague, who reads the news every hour, now links the melodies with verses of his own. 'There's something here for everyone/We'll keep the music coming fast tonight/For every taste under the sun/ We've got the rhythm that is right.' But on no account have power! Over nobody. Power in any form is ridiculous and detestable, even in the most cramped corner, even—and above all—in love, where one so quickly goes into the descendant in the eyes of the other.

'Give me a call!' she suddenly cries down there, 'let me know what you're doing! How you are. Don't shut me out!'

He, despondent, looks out of the window at the Golgotha of

[24]

the television aerials across on the roof of the Landesbank. Its dark scobalite begins to reflect. High up, dusty yellow clouds with waving frays flow by. A man doesn't need a woman. A man needs no one. She became so dependent on him and his every utterance that she even adopted his contemptuous views on women and parroted them to degrade other women, utterly dispossessed. These women have never experienced a lower depth than à *deux*.

She calls again from down below. 'I want to make my peace with you, that's all, just make my peace with you. I can't go like this.'

He is embarrassed in front of his neighbours; it is five in the morning. One ought to call the police . . . Oh God, how pitiful! This damned lying world of *relationships*! Snaps the healthiest soul, snaps the healthiest urge.

Before the painter's eyes scenes and changing images rise. On the fringe of a riding tournament on a Sunday afternoon. His girlfriend in a circle of new women-friends he doesn't know. In another group not far away her beloved (he himself) to whom she looks across, her arms folded beneath her bosom, as if she were looking across the boxing ring, in the midst of her seconds, to her opponent in the heaviest weight class. She sizes him up clearly, coolly, classically. Her darling, in his circle, cracks a joke. But as he does so he looks over to her and examines her set expression. This virtuous, familiar face of his girlfriend is suddenly masked by something like the visor of a helmet behind which someone unknown lives and peers out. An elderly woman on her staff gives her one last piece of advice: block, clutch, save up your strength. The combatant woman nods. The hatred is unwavering, the alien look, the will to attack. Nevertheless, this round too goes to him on points. The woman stumbles back to her corner to be seen to. Her women-friends bend over her, speak encouragingly to her, change tactics. They now ask whether she feels strong enough to fight for a decision still in this next, late round. In her corner the woman nods her hanging head and says, wailing: 'Yes, yes'. Whether she feels up to opening with an

[25]

attack all of a sudden, to penetrate his cover at half distance? Yes, yes, the battered one nods, and cries pitifully, immersed in the emptiness of an interval in the fight. An interval in which her life rushes down her in a torrent . . .

Now she lies across the bonnet of the white Citroën, her head buried in her elbow, and has finally fallen asleep, it seems. Sleep, sleep! . . . Soon you will be sharing your joys and sorrows with someone else. Believe me, from one day to the next you will move over into someone else's biography and will once again happily settle in there as if in a new house and the morning after the first night you will already take the crockery from his kitchen cupboard without further ado, as if it had always been yours.

Now you have got sleepy, Grit. Your listening has led me here and now soothes me. Listening is a beautiful submission and the only dignified kind. But very, very few know that. Nowadays you can narrate what you want, you can offer up your innermost self, it will only lead to someone next to you continually nodding, more and more restlessly confirming you and above all himself, hardly paying any more attention to your words and only burning to counter that he too has already experienced the same, the very same thing . . . So let us be silent. But first let us go down to the canal, before your tired head becomes too heavy, and sit by the water. Not go home yet . . .

There, where the helicopter winks its red dot in the half-light, the city freeway flows into the west end and the long Sunday evening jam begins. (The traffic patrol can see you all!) In the canal the reflections of the bank lanterns quiver. 'Aglaia', the old pleasure barge, returns empty and aglow after the last coffee afternoon trip to its mooring. On deck two couples are still dancing under colourful bulbs. One of them, father and mother who have wearily found each other; the other, the long-suffering kids, two girls, who totter in aping paces beside their parents, who now take no notice of them,

[26]

and for their part, just for a joke, preserve a tender peace for a bit. Below in the bar all the tables have already been cleared and two lean old waiters sit doing their accounts and smoking cigars.

Since Joseph moved out Grit has no longer felt quite at home in her flat. It is getting too large for her now. Three and a half rooms in an old building, two of them very spacious, with high ceilings, swallow up one person on her own. To have too much unoccupied space around you makes you lonely and insecure, just as too great a confinement drives you crazy.

For this reason she welcomes her father's wanting to stay in town and finds it convenient to take him in temporarily. It will doubtless be good, she thinks, if the rooms have more life in them. And above all if someone is there in the evenings waiting for her. By all means let her father take up his quarters there. Mind you, he must take things as they come; he could help here and there in the travel agency.

Joseph, an archivist in the state photographic department, who is always listening to records and never seems fully awake, had tired her within a year, simply by too much peace. In everything he was gentle and mild, never offered resistance, at most a shrug of the shoulders if something wasn't to his liking. Although older than Grit, he nonetheless seemed in a strange way not to have grown up. He had wrapped himself up in his wine-red velvet trousers, his jacket embroidered with colourful silk flowers and all kinds of patches, his shoulder-length curled hair, the whole beatific benevolence of the early years. A quiet but still a somewhat sinister *déjà-vu* figure from a long-gone youth movement, who has made himself implacably at home in his twentieth year and to this day prefers playing Vanilla Fudge once more to getting accustomed to new LPs by Ted Nugent or Rainbow.

Rifts, tumult, violence and unrest, sudden shoves of un-restrained life under your soles, the old feeling of wellbeing that you had with long quiet pieces of music shattered, the object of your wishes again undefined . . . You take the record off: not this music ever again. Never! You jump up from your cinema seat and leave the laid–back, leisurely film. This piece of work has not been tried in combat, for you it is neither incentive nor opponent. In conversations now you frequently notice ghostly clever–cleverness that belongs to a long-faded way of thinking and has nothing to contribute to the altered position of mysteries. You travel to a place you often visited earlier and would like to kick it: wake up, you lazy place! Your cheeks, your hills are getting chapped, your evening breeze chars and stinks. It may be that tomorrow you will already be the gateway to a deep descent! . . . Grit too experiences an unconscious recoil from what was and from things to come and can no longer feel satisfied with Joseph and his sagging rapture. Something in her has split off, and of a sudden she says, ingenuously and firmly determined: 'I'm looking for someone with strengths that I don't yet know. Someone for a change who speaks a completely different language.'

Now they sit in the Big Room that looks out on the quiet street, her father in the armchair in front of the dainty bureau, Grit on the floor, where some hundred of the travel industry's brochures and catalogues lie scattered about. Her father is to pick a trip, for relaxation and for one last breather before his final return to the Institute. Grit gives him good tips galore, advises him patiently on Sunday afternoon, and, in doing so, avails herself uninhibitedly of the same agreeable phrases she uses to make the Algarve or Bangkok appealing for strangers in her agency. But nothing quite appeals to her father. He turns away from the brochures and looks out of the window. For a long time they say nothing about this decision which can in no way be taken. A sycamore wing with its seed dangling flies past the window as if it were alive, like an insect bearing a burden, from one tree to the next, is caught up there and does not twirl down to the ground.

'What on earth am I to do? What on earth am I to do?' her father asks, gazing out, and sucks in a deep sigh through his lips.

'You really don't know what to do with yourself, do you?' Grit, slightly aggrieved, leafs through the travel supplement of a glossy magazine and idly drops it again, since her effort is hardly worth it in face of so much listlessness.

Slowly and hesitantly her father begins to speak of how much he misses Zachler; how indispensable to him his position of enmity toward this man is. This man who is forever better, whom he always revolts against, who nonetheless always spurred him on to the highest exertion of his powers. Now he finds himself totally isolated and cut off from this man whom he would almost call his mortal enemy—and you never abandon such an enemy before the struggle has really been fought to the last. Yet he fears that his own strength will be waning, his fighting spirit weakening, since he cannot get near him. 'He has cut me off completely from his sphere,' says her father. 'Even if I returned to the Institute today or tomorrow I would have to take up so insignificant a position there that I couldn't get at Zachler at all or only in ludicrous skirmishes from a position of awful inferiority. In life you can only come across such an opponent once, who makes it worthwhile to keep at the peak of your powers—and reputation!—and probably that is an even rarer treasure than what they call the love of a lifetime.'

In how many superiors has he not sought an opponent of sufficient weight to replace a Zachler, he says. But either they were not prepared to enter into a struggle or those who were prepared were each and every one bogey men or no more than smoothly-functioning heads without charges, without charisma.

Most recently of all once more in Oldenburg. The state government had commissioned a study of the desertion of city centres. He went, left the Institute, not least because immediately after the scholarship there was the prospect of a permanent teaching position. During the work the project

[29]

leader was amply tested by him for his suitability as an enemy. Nothing came of it, the man always amiably let him have his way, however intolerantly and muddle-headedly her father behaved. Instead he must have intrigued against him behind his back, for the teaching position was not assigned in the end, contrary to expectation. You had such windbags in the way of superiors often enough!

In the few days her father has been with her Grit has already been observing how changes are visible in his face, how the skin has become paler and more wrinkled. His mouth often droops somewhat slackly. His eyes have a silky sheen, seem open for everything at a distance but weary of anything within reach, which, by the by, includes the most basic duties in their shared flat, and even personal hygiene. He is fairly letting himself go. At times it seems as if a part of his being and of his body too had leapt ahead in a sudden start into old age. Sometimes he speaks unclearly and incoherently, even when he is not at all drunk. Then what he says creeps closely along the border of semi-consciousness and idiocy. Only the strange thing is this: that at such moments you think you are perceiving a decline in his familiar powers as well as at the same time an upsurge in hitherto unknown powers of his spirit.

'What shall I do? What shall I do?' he laments a second time, and what this is supposed to mean is: how am I to get at Zachler again, at the enemy, how—dismissed and sent away from there, demoted here, with neither a position nor a front—how am I to resume the fight with such seriousness and finality as it must now have?

Her father gets up from the armchair and stands at the window. He looks out and entwines his hands firmly behind his coccyx. 'Only hatred unites. Hatred, hatred, always be up front, always be the first.'

Grit opens all the brochures on Tunisia once again. She says softly, as she reads: 'That is absolutely evil.'

This was spoken so matter-of-factly and her voice was so devoid of purpose that her father continues to hear her for a long time. The little simple sentence has so much space to it that he loses himself in it for a long time, just as at times you can hear deep down into a person through a certain hollowness in speech. He goes round the armchair once and sits in it again. Grit is still squatting on the floor amid the many brochures, comparing prices and what is offered.

Thus it remains for hours. Sometimes they gaze at length into each other's eyes while each of them thinks along his own lines.

Strong natures of great firmness, of great brutality even, if once they have been properly shaken, seem to sink heavier and deeper into despondency than nervous weaklings do. Bekker—since he constantly waits without will in the armchair and cannot decide to do anything—again feels the burden of that big cadaver which in him became nameless as 'the officer' and became the very image of the human ability to be manly and indescribably unhappy. The officer, who liked telling the boy—above all when the latter was treating his bouts of melancholy thoughtlessly—about those astonishing cases of death caused by nothing other than a mere wounding of honour or some offence. He took richly elaborated portrayals of spiritual deaths from an old travel account which took you to the warlike tribes of Oceania and paid particular attention to the New Zealand Maoris. For the Maori—a cheerful and courageous warrior, a man of highly developed moral concepts, full of a subtle sense of doubt and an extraordinary physical stamina—the Maori could be felled by a single humiliation and dropped into an apathy from which there was no way out. *Pure* apathy spread from the spirit into all the body's organs, the movements of muscles went to sleep and within a few days he died through failure of the vagus. . . . Had not the old fellow then died like a Maori of wounded honour? And was perhaps nothing else to be his own destiny. What's up, old chap? Do you see me still and remain silent because I went wrong and disappointed you?—I see that you are in a miserable way, my boy, yes. I see too that you will be in a far more miserable condition in those years to come that still remain to you. But still I don't know whether I should

[31]

advise you to go on running after me—as far as here. I cannot help you, and I cannot advise you. Death has made me an observer without judgement. As one of the dead I know and see more of life than the living, but of death I can say as little as I could say of life when I was alive. . . .

'You don't want to go to Holland?' asks Grit, and holds up two picture pages. 'Holland, Holland,' murmurs Bekker, and does not know what the word should make him think of. The room is so empty. Only the armchair and the bureau and the floor. No pictures on the white walls. No table, no table-cloth. . . . Even the shelves built into the walls are empty. Joseph has taken away what was his. All you can do is let your thoughts wander across the parquet, along the stern ornamentation of the rhombuses. The wood is blunt and cracked.

Below in the street a small boy just out of the cinema runs by on his way home from the 5th galaxy. His broken arm, which sticks out awkwardly from his chest, is in a splint and plaster, forced through shirt and pullover. Rigidly posed like this in a position of fearful self-defence, he cannot feel anything properly, cannot raise any of the good feelings of the cinema in his small body. Only he plays incessantly and nervously with his fingers, which peep out of the top of the plaster tube: the impatient finger exercises of a piano pupil who has already had to miss too many lessons. What a delay at the age of ten—to be in plaster for weeks on end! He is beset by the fear that all the rest of him will grow and grow and only the arm that has been yoked to the plaster and crammed into it will remain smaller.

'You really don't want to go anywhere, father.'

Grit crouches kneeling and mixes up the brochures. Then she bends forward and lets her head sink slowly on to the paper. Her left temple presses into the Bundesbahn's winter timetable. Her hip sticks up high. Her right eye, fixed and mild, watches her father.

'Yes I do. But where?'

The trip ought to be A River. Home and foreign parts, going on and staying the same, One Current. Without

[32]

changing, waits or stopovers. The only thing you'd really like is to drift downstream like Moses in his basket and sometime be fished out by someone or other, shortly before it is too late. To wake up on another continent among grinning junkies, washed up on a little island, bang in the centre of the crossroads of two boulevards, where seats stand under three dirty palms and close as sparrows the addicts sit who now, after all the bottles and injections, are numbed by sniffed exhaust fumes. Occasionally one twitches wildly and threatens the spirits that haunt him. Most of the time, though, they are semi-conscious and seem to be being caressed by the noise as others on a beach let the surf caress them. Once a young woman leaps to her feet and shouts at her friend, into his face, that he should finally make some movement again. He sits on the island all day long, with mulish open eyes, hours without any movement. The woman nags and pushes him, demands that he move a little, right this minute. She hits him, is beside herself. It is as if she sensed: this is irrevocably the last moment, right now! she can still pull back her friend from the final endless downward whirl. Daily she keeps a careful watch over his fixed trance, without, however, being able to do anything about his distances. Now she has succeeded in catching him by means of blows and shouts, and far in the distance something in him stirs. But hardly has he come round even a little before his first impulse is to look round for his buddies, because in front of them he is embarrassed by the loud scolding of his girlfriend, embarrassed because they are all seeking peace here by the street sea. Just back from the shadows, and his first not indifferent glance squints fearfully after the others, to see what they may be thinking of him. Then he permits her to draw him to his feet and he shambles away somewhat shakily on his girlfriend's arm. The woman immediately becomes quite calm and contented. The veins standing out from yelling, the folds from nagging, are gone from one moment to the next. Satisfaction, unconsidered, with an unhappiness that remains constant in her whole face, beside her man who is moving again.

It wears you down, not being able to reach a decision. The travel world grows ever more impassable. Fantasy pushes ahead in a direction that forks off from each and every destination. Why go away at all? It's nice here with Grit. A little bleak and uncomfortable, but nice enough.

After all, thinks Bekker, you consider—the older you get—the places along the way more and more often in the light of whether you'd like to stop by here or would find it intensely disagreeable to stay here of all places. You examine them as you try on shoes; you adjust your head to an interesting view; feel whether it is comfortable or not; wonder whether something gentle would be better or something rugged, open spaces or cosy confinement . . . country or city.

Apart from anything else, there is only one true destination for Bekker's travels: the boss's floor in Behrendstrasse, office number one, where even at the weekend, when no one is there, the ceiling light burns discreetly, where a certain Zachler will one day leap up behind his desk scared to death when Bekker pulls open the door and rushes in and stands before him as no other . . .

Grit still cowers strangely contorted on the floor, like a wild cat in a cage, surrendering to all-powerful indolence with her posterior pushed out and her head turned. Her mouth is a little open. That fine depression above the upper lip, which at one time was called the snot-groove, now of course always clean and covered with a fine down of light hairs—it would be hard today to find an appropriate name for this small, significant mark of her beauty. Around the mouth and chin her features are conspicuously mixed as well; a remainder of undefined form, something of childlike abjectness, is present there too in that face whose upper half has developed clarity and a penetrating gaze. Her father suddenly stands up, and, seemingly stretching his legs, walks briskly to and fro along the wall with the two high windows. But stolen glances and a cramped smile betray that while walking he is only calculating how he can get out of his tracks again—and featherlight, as it were without premeditation and quite of his own accord, come down to that mouth and that region down there. There is nothing else for it but for him to bend down somewhat laboriously and slide across to Grit on his knees and fists. Her eye, watching him, rises slowly as he approaches till it is at its uppermost angle. To bring his face into alignment with hers he has to jack-knife his arms low down, which sends the blood to his head, the veins in his forehead standing out thick as roots, his elbows beginning to tremble. Entry into that open mouth under the open eye—so hollow, so soft, so hospitable, and yet no more than if he were entering another empty room. He slinks on tongue-tip forward and back again; nothing moves. That was the kiss. In the position of the drowsy face he has altered nothing nor given the observing eye anything to do or even cause to blink. Her father hops from his knees on to his feet and stretches to full height. He shoves both hands under his jacket pockets into his trousers and puffs a few nervous bars of an undefined melody in the air. Now he does not return to the armchair but instead leans against the window-sill, from where he can look at Grit's parting, without her eye seeing him. She raises herself, groaning and chirping, and sitting on her calves loosens two pins from her hair and sticks them in her mouth. (That same mouth! That mouth that can cope so well with everything . . .) With both hands she loosens her long hair and secures it with the pins behind her ears.

'I remember,' she says, 'that the two of us took a holiday at the Mondsee once, when I was in junior fifth.' She stands up and sits in the armchair before the bureau. She crosses her legs and folds her hands over her knees.

'Yes,' says her father, 'I remember it well. That time at the Mondsee.' Before his eyes, however, there suddenly arise images of devastation and he hardly remembers. From their round mobile snack-bar at the most northerly end of town, father and daughter, in silvery-grey protective clothing, step out into the eternal sandstorm.

But they only reel and totter on the spot, ponderously try to hop, hand in hand. Beneath their feet a splitting scraping, as if whole plates of the earth were shoving on top of each other.

There they are: tumult, the fool and his wife . . .

Grit, walking beside me, plunging into the water, abusing and provoking me, malicious and tender, my child, of long ago, now at last I love her. Tumult, a hollow rumbling, repeated babbling, rumour. Something is brewing. The order of things resembles the speech of a child allowed to stay up too late at night: the nonos are coming, the noughts and the nines, every creature that's been born, in fact, the nonos, the nos. The imbeciles are coming, the predatory men in hordes and armies, each side shoving the other off the globe, and it will be just as if all at once on a full-day-opening Saturday the sound of doomsday rings out and in the department store those who have risen from the dead also push into the throng, to buy with the greatest of greed, these abstemious ones! . . . Tired after the long night of the ball, the magnificent gala evening that followed upon the Creation, God the Almighty has fallen asleep in slippers and top hat on the steps of his palace. But in the palm of his hand the tribes of man creep and crawl about, and when next day he awakens he shakes them off him in disgust and tramples on them in his slippers . . .

Bekker, pointing respectively into the distance, to his own heart and to Grit, says: 'There they are: tumult, the fool and his wife . . .'

'What?' asks Grit. 'I don't get you.'

Her father repeats the three words and the gesture with his hand.

She laughs, somewhat at a loss: 'Wife? . . . Me?'

Her father looks dejectedly down at the floor. 'Yes,' he says softly.

Grit, her legs crossed, swings her right foot round and round manifestly faster.

PENSION 'Anschütz', to the east of the Mondsee and above it, is still there, yes. The hosts are still the same too, healthy and grown older in contentment. Not Austrians but Swabians; they have assiduously kept up with the times and have installed a solarium, sauna, and swimming-pool with bar in the cellars, so that now you have to pay some three hundred schillings for a single room, in the off-season. They even think they can remember—Bekker, yes of course, such a young man and already he had so big a daughter, it must be ten years or more ago already. Presumably what they remember is above all that unforgettably noisy weekend when Grit's mother came to stay and arguments and shouting resounded through the lightly-built house day and night. There was beating and screaming on account of her friend—at that time newly acquired, someone from her Protestant work-group, an ethnologist, a researcher into fairy tales!—who then even picked her up here, soon after Bekker had once again hit her hard a few times and Grit's mother tottered red and weepy out of the door while he stood at the window and was excited at putting himself in the position of the strange man who now received this abused and humbled woman, this big woman with no trace of wretchedness about her, with long legs and broad shoulders, marked with bloody weals and running abrasions, her hair twisted, but what a touching power emanated from that beautiful, beaten-down body as it walked away . . . Oh damn, the footprints of this long-gone struggle are everywhere on the floor here still, invisible prints overlaid a hundred times on this cheap matting runner . . . Well, the two of them then drove down to Yugoslavia in his old Volvo, it being summer then. Now, on the other hand, it is mid-November. Snow is already falling as low as a height of eight

[37]

hundred metres. A dismal season of the year, unwholesome
for going out, for taking walks. You can hardly see a thing.
Not even the Mondsee, which after all is right in front of the
house, can be properly made out; since Bekker's arrival it has
been enveloped in dense fog. You could in fact be somewhere
quite different here. At four in the afternoon it is already pitch
dark and Herr Anschütz switches on the television downstairs
in the breakfast-room. Bekker has come on ahead alone, by
plane to Salzburg and then by train. Grit has to accustom
Joseph to the work back home, as he is to take her place in the
travel agency for the next few weeks. Presumably they have
again eased the barrier of separation between them a little . . .
Bekker often sits from midday onward in his room and drinks
large quantities of cognac. At this time of year, which travel
agents rightly call the dead season, hardly anyone feels like
going to the Mondsee, and he is the only guest in the pension.
Although, this being so, he would have sole run of the facilities
in the cellars, he makes no use of them, and in addition seeks as
little contact as possible with the family, who live on the first
floor.

Here it truly is unbearable, says Bekker, and snaps on the
overhead light, the spider-armed, ugly lamp above the bed—a
more unbearable, more dismal corner is barely conceivable.
Why did the child shove me off down here? Why do I have to
sit here alone in this damp, cold holiday dungeon? . . . I'm
tired of it, Grit. The place is wrong, the lodgings are wrong,
the whole trip is wrong, even my walk this morning, which
was to refresh me, was a total failure. I ended up in a
completely pathless woodcutters' clearing barricaded with
stumps and branches, and stumbled about up to my ankles in
snow. It was steep, steeper and steeper further up the
mountain, and over the mountain was where I wanted to go.
But every path petered out; I wandered about in light summer
shoes through Nature's rubbish, froze and immediately got
my shooting pains in the prostate. The wood at that height
was misty and spooky. Alert to danger as I never am down
below on level ground, on roads, I stopped more and more

frequently, to listen to things that the snapping under my soles was perhaps drowning out. Nothing, though, as good as nothing. The entire upper forest yawningly empty. Only towards the end, as I descended once more hither and thither among the trunks and already supposed I had gone a good deal out of my way, I heard the cries of jays, turned in their direction and saw that they were circling above that very turn in the path from which I had started my aimless and utterly uninteresting ascent. Walking in open country weighs upon my spirits, deadens me. It is hardly possible to think peacefully about anything. The variety of the species and forms of Nature, the edge of the paths that trammel me, do not permit it. Unswerving in the face of incontestable advice or law, there is not enough leeway for one's own ideas left. So I shall soon march straight ahead, blind and whistling. Looking back, however, I feel dizzy and fit to spew when I remember this bloodlessness in the head, this blankness, this mere walking walking . . . It was otherwise, though, the day before, when I travelled to Salzburg and, also without any particular interest, wandered the narrow streets there. But from this walking amid walls, history and stench there arose a throbbing awareness and willpower which at length intensified into an ungovernable urge for a hitherto unknown physical aberration, an orgasm of fighting from which there might be no more awakening. Every pace was suddenly a trembling step in Zachler's direction . . . Where to, with so much energy? There is only the overthrow of society as the next greatest thing to moving mountains . . . And then this little chicken of a late-night-radio editor flaps across to my table, his name is Ludwig and I know him by sight, from the pubs back home; he sits down with me and snuffles at my opinions, makes a few captious comments on the latest acts of violence, which goodness knows were no mere paperbag bangs. His eyes grow quite fearfully uncomprehending if you interpose some reservation—brown eyes and sadly afraid that he might not understand or might be seen in the wrong light. Suddenly he makes a face, a grin of the most clandestine zeal, and shows his front teeth, mouldy from smoking: 'And the anarchists? What do you think of them? They are an amazing bunch, when you come to think of it, an amazing bunch.' And the blushing red of a forbidden passion, a fierce glow, appears in his pale skin. How could I agree with this feeble enthusiast? I have to contradict him, even if in doing so I am forced to advocate the exact opposite of my actual opinion! . . . Brokdorf, he says later. All he says is Brokdorf, repeatedly, and in his staring gaze summons forth scenes of a great battle. That aside, he has now got to the stage of needing an experience of genuine solidarity again, and for this reason is travelling in the next day or so via Salzburg and Vienna to the anarchist congress in Barcelona . . . The assassins, who commit crimes—for whom? for the ignorant people?—do their inevitable business without anyone commissioning them, simply in the name of breaking, negating, doing. War against Now can only mean: in this and in no other way. No after and no Utopia. Shots across the cake, kidnapping, blows, shocks and terror. Quite right if some feel it is high time to do evil, to do what is irrevocably evil. When, if not before the absoluteness of evil-doing, would we be capable of more profoundly recognizing or doubting the nature of our community? There are hours ruled by an immense spirit of ice, and then hatred is the only warmth and only exploding the limits can enable you to draw breath. Hence the perverse holiness of murderers, of the unthinking evildoers who do not even think of themselves, however mute their deeds may be, however little they may proclaim; after all, young kids hardly know how to put two words together, they copy both good and bad from the secret messages of their ancestors. In geometrical measuring and mathematical calculation, in the perfect administration of their deeds, they will soon already be secret spiritual brothers of that very power and state machinery they aim to destroy. And yet even their coldest, most perfect *coups de main* preserve a residue of that rebellion, that wildness of terror, which alone is still trying today to cause the iron round-dance of planners and makers, exploiters and exploited,

[40]

love and lying, progress and destruction, to stumble for a moment, maybe to stop short. For that, for one vague, tiny moment of faltering, they have to throw the entire weight of the world's moral judgement that they are evil, senseless and cruel into the balance. This morality they have at all events been able to bear for a while . . . The state, which wishes to settle—properly settle—with anyone and everyone that opposes it as the power of the Totally Other, which always knows how to make a devil of you, displace you—it has found its sinister master, its first unswallowable resistance, in a small, stammering élite' of haters who have driven a few bloody ghosts into its sleep. It is perhaps the last of the old struggles. Or perhaps the first of the new: against the limitless, frontless uniformity and levelness of politics, of aimlessly teeming life. Is it an act of decay or an act of birth? The directions are indistinguishable: forward/back, blind/seeing, left/right. A clod, like the soul itself. A ball of dirt, like the earth itself, that a sacred scarab rolls through the ether. . . . One thing is certain; the old decisions are no longer valid. For that reason each one of us know-it-alls will utter hoarse cries in every direction now, we are in the bush again. Every one in his field, gone newly primitive and tangle-haired, every one will first have to give up some of his own harmlessness . . . Perhaps I am already too old, though, and resemble the blunt block of wood which is no longer so well able to rebel in the fire as a light piece. Yes, that may be. But the rose of explosion, the rose of the root, when once it opens you will be astounded, you Ludwigs everywhere . . . I must get down to the lowest flowers, deep under the sand and the cities' hummocks. But it is repellent to sense the convulsive recoil of a whole people in your own body, to be One Flesh with all of them, with healthy reflexes, when one of these national acts of terror explodes and shakes Mr. Average to his idle bone and marrow . . . How many pleasures still, till we are finally thoroughly rotten? . . . I want to remain cold toward such paroxysms and clamours and in the most national moment feel a light sensation between my shoulder-blades, the counter-balance: a warm ray of sunshine that plays on you as you stand shakily at the wash-stand and the glittering water leaps across the back of your hand and a thousand kilometres to the south, in the lagoon, a tiny tug, generously helpful, hauls through the canal a Goliath of a tanker which, powerless, silently and submissively glides on, and the houses on the opposite bank are so humbly small behind its Great Back . . . Politics is trying to pee highest in public. It is only a matter of who can jet the most piss the furthest. The assassins all have a kink in their jet. Those aspiring to power, the ambitious, Herostratuses, arsonists. Imperturbably the researcher into instinctual impulses contemplates the rebellious Thumberling: do what you consider right. You will never cease to be the object of my boundless understanding . . . Everywhere the police blow whistles and urge on their dogs, the rapid-fire guns stare. The entire state is as rigid and stiff as an animal scented out. Fists balled at the seam of its trousers, full of impotent rage. Public rationality becoming more and more immature, a curious regression into the childlike. Public language, its circum-spection heavily armour-plated. And if only someone in public would dare to consider a little and let his thoughts wander freely a little—he would necessarily grow dizzy on the spot, so that his speech would be a tumbling confusion and he would needs lament out loud and accuse himself of lying. Instead, this immature creature acts as if he were master of the situation and sees to it that his wargame toys have made a loud noise once, and are loaded . . . Oh no! Be sure you see and hear nothing more. It disgusts me. Who else should I listen to? Businessmen or civil servants? Childen or sportsmen? The hunters or the hunted? The teachers, judges or the tramps of the city? Women among themselves, or TV artistes? Who can you still listen to? The Deutschs around me here are none of them the real thing. The Deutschs of humanity are so . . . I don't know . . . so closed. A rattling sound, and it's cut off. Linguistic overcrowded areas. Only get out of here! Out of language. . . ! I don't want to hear or see any more. Rather live than scrape by. Rather be like an empty flagpole atop an abandoned embassy villa than a bird or other such nonsense. Or a gecko in the desert, which can wipe its goggle-eyes with its own tongue . . . I'm a patriot, but I don't know who I should turn to. Where is the lord and master my devotion demands?

Five days later Grit comes. She has driven for over ten hours through fog and rain in her Peugeot, and reaches the Mondsee late in the evening. She finds the pension on the hillside without trouble, once she has passed through the village and turned into the Uferstrasse. Every return starts her heart beating hard, and so does this one, to a small, dark holiday spot where houses and shops have stood still since her childhood. The pension hosts greet her cordially but without the demonstrative heartiness which during the drive she had anticipated as the cosier, the tireder she grew. But for Herr and Frau Anschütz it is not in the first instance a reunion: they do not recognize the little Grit of those days in this adult young woman, basically—in spite of playing pick-sticks together all those rained-off afternoons—they remember only dimly. So their first impression is of her standing strangely awkward before them, twisting her neck and clutching her elbows because of a suppressed embrace. She is told that her father is eating his evening meal in the village, as he generally does at this time. Frau Anschütz adds to this information a little and really somewhat impertinent sigh, as if she had a good deal to put up with, with some of Grit's father's ways. Grit, since she is hungry and very tired after the journey, decides to drive over to the village right away, without unpacking first and refreshing herself in her room. Nor does she trouble to spend a long time hunting for her father in the various inns, as they will be meeting later at the pension in any case. For the rest, she is a little disappointed that he has done nothing at all by way of receiving her, has not even left a message as to where he can be found.

She turns into the Schwarzer Bär, descends to the long vaulted cellarage of the dining-hall with its many niches and corners, where in former days she was allowed to sit with her father late into the night dicing for bear-gums, Asterix figures and candied almonds. And with the scent of wood, beer and damp walls she suddenly knows in all her senses how it was when she tormented her father here ten years ago to buy her at last a first pair of jeans. The time and location and nature of this small, powerful covetousness are for a fraction of a second genuine and vivid and disrupt the present totally. A little later she notices in the waitress, from whom she orders a beef heart in sour-cream sauce, an odd habit she knows very well from someone else, the small but disconcerting idiosyncrasy of frowning and drawing up her eyebrows, pulling a face to attract interest. It is precisely the same expression that an elderly customer of Grit's always puts on when she is listening. Yes, exactly like old Frau zur Leyen! The very image of her, and copied from her, for she has been spending her summer holidays here at the Mondsee for many years. A brow like that looks as if it is always doubting you, as if it has doubts about what you are going to order, about anything you might say. In truth, however, it means nothing more than that she is slightly hard of hearing, at all events in old Frau zur Leyen's case, and behind the refined and apparently sceptical forehead she pricks up her weak ears very acutely. It must be a catching tic, and no doubt the waitress got it by waiting on the old woman a lot, and so it now grafts an amount of stubbornness and depth on to her cute face. Grit props her throbbing head in both hands: in it the ribbons of road continue to thread along and the first creatures of sleep come riding in to her overtaxed senses. Not welcomed and quite exhausted, she all at once feels very left alone and exposed in this loud cave of a village evening.

Across from her sit a group of youngish businessmen at their regular table. Representatives or agents, at any rate employees of a larger estate agency that operates a branch in the neighbourhood, for at times they talk of the top-level board of directors as of something at a great distance, geographically speaking too. True, they speak in an Upper Austrian dialect, but it sounds dressed up and no longer much

[44]

at home, smoothed-out and stretched by a lot of business German. You hear them mentioning certain property transactions, certain plans, loan agreements, referring in the process to Leitz files which every one of them carries with him and which contain photos and ground plans in plastic sleeves. One with a round bare skull and flat sideboards leads the conversation and collects the reports. He is the boss and sits at the top of the table too, to which all the other heads are turned as soon as he opens his mouth, and even when he is silent, reading papers, one of them will be observing him in secret consideration of leadership powers. Once he refers to a Doctor Spantel or Prantel and asks where he is. Instantly a diligent disquiet goes round the whole table, and like tale-telling little girls the employees compete in criticizing the improbable unpunctuality of their colleague. One after the other they pitch into him, and each of them is able to present a particularly inadequate quality in the doctor. Finally the boss announces with an expression of embarrassment, indeed of affected mourning, that the colleague at the centre of the contention has by now been as good as given up by the top-rank directors of the firm. Given up! he says; not, say, that notice is being served on him, but that he has been 'given up' as doctors give up a patient terminally ill. Thereupon they all start clamouring anew and interrupting each other, stress their personal deep regret, call the management's decision hard but unavoidable, and then once again get off their chests—now with no restraint whatsoever—all the things they have never been able to stomach about the doctor. At this moment their belated colleague comes hurrying in, he who has been given up stands there in person before them—you know at once that this must be him by the way they all instantly clam up and swallow the remains of their nasty defamation. The doctor, a slim, nervous man, long past middle age, is not wearing the suit that is usual in conferences and customer service, as does each of his younger colleagues, but instead a pullover and knee-length breeches. Only the Leitz file tucked under his arm indicates that he has come prepared for an official session. His right hand holds his little daughter, a girl of eight or nine years of age. All those at the table stare in pale horror at the child. No doubt this evening is the first time they have set eyes on her. She has only one arm. The right, half-length sleeve of her dirndl dress hangs flat and empty from her shoulder. Her father turns first to the boss. He makes his excuses. He apologizes for being late and for having to bring the little one along. Her mother, however, decided at short notice to leave for her sister's in Salzburg, and he didn't want the child to stay worried at home . . . Without hesitating, without her father's needing to tell her, plunging as it were headfirst into the waves of false pity or horror that always flood over her from strangers, the girl starts greeting every one of the men, one after the other. She looks very well-behaved and yet seems to function according to some inner mechanism, almost greedily, as if the little one were collecting gifts with every shake of her hand. She curtseys and extends the one arm, the left, as if she were stretching it out for her fingertips to be kissed, but without meeting anyone's eyes in doing so, indeed, her eyes are almost screwed shut. Some of the employees even raise their backsides from their seats a little as she does this, uncertain as to the honour a healthy adult should pay an invalid child. When the boss cannot take his secret gaze from the little one and a pinched smile remains below his eyes, the girl's father bows to him and again excuses himself one last time, now for his little daughter as a whole. He says: 'Please excuse the way it looks. . .'.

Grit spits a lump of chewed-up meat on to her plate. She is close to vomiting right over the table.

The girl snuggles up against her father's hip. The round of greetings has if anything made her even more shy. The boss makes room next to him on the seat for the one they've given up and his child. Both of them sit down and the father opens his file, ready for work. Since he doesn't know what is required at present he smooths a plastic sleeve at random with the back of his hand. Magnified and horrible as everything happening at the next table appears to Grit in her overwrought

[46]

condition, she would like most of all to leap across and drag this sad toady to the floor by his collar. This perverse failure!—dragging his crippled child along to generate sympathy and favour for himself, and then, when he notices that the effect is more horror-stricken than moved, he detaches himself from the child, please excuse the way it looks!—as if he were speaking of a mangy cur, of a slovenly room full of dirty laundry. Does he not notice at all how his position has already ruined him to the bottom of his heart and how he continues to hang on his boss's every word and has no notion that the top level have long given him up. . . . I heard it along with the rest, thinks Grit, I shall go over and explain it all to him. . . . 'You shit, you,' she breathes softly.

At that moment a drunk runs right through the hall, races by so as not to stagger, and at the agents' table flops into a chair that one of the employees has just vacated.

Grit has already known from hearing that racing, those runaway tripping steps. Her father. Only he runs like that, and when he does he is so drunk that he is not quite straight in his head. He can't get out a word any more; just these steps, these mincing steps, he hardly hears, he races about and seems to be fleeing invisible pursuers. Now at the table his concern is to fold together his heavy legs and arms, he tries to sit low and inconspicuously, so that his pursuers might perhaps fail to spot him . . . So he has been here in the cellar all along, and presumably was drinking in a back corner with strangers. But this little old man—and in a traditional-style jacket! Grit is startled to find her father so weirdly transformed, as if he had passed on to another age of life, another homeland with strange customs and costumes. No, she tells herself, he is just crouched up now, and his whole stature is out of joint with drinking. But why does he buy himself such a silly jacket! He looks with timorously wide-open eyes under the table and places his hands firmly on his knees, really intending his presence not to be noticeable.

'Evening, Herr Bekker,' the smartly-turned-out men say to her father, a little jovially but without condescension, since

[47]

even this holiday guest could be a property client tomorrow. The little girl with only one arm huddles up to her father, howling. She is afraid of the drunk, the stiff, silent guest, and cries out to her father in a blubbering voice to chase the Nasty Man away. At this, Grit's outrage is of a sudden directed against this whiningly super-sensitive kid, who abuses Grit's father (sitting there absently and helplessly), kicking up a fuss as if the Erlking were after her . . . Shut it, you little beast . . . Freak!

Making a visible effort, the drunk once again suddenly rises to his feet. In doing so he knocks the chair over behind him. He trips along in a dashing curve across the stone flags and comes to a stop right at Grit's table. The racket of the toppled chair seems somehow to cling to him; he keeps his right hand, with which he last touched the chair as he stood up, against his back and opens and shuts it repeatedly, as if trying to grab hold of the fallen backrest.

'Father,' Grit says softly.

The drunk with his tired, sorrowful eyes bows slightly as innkeepers do when they welcome dinner guests. Then, swaying and no longer at the double, he returns to the table where he earlier wasted the evening drinking in the company of a group of young men, hockey-players, whose noise has already been booming across to Grit the whole time. But she wasn't to know that that crowd were using her father for their jokes.

So now she had had her greeting. Probably her father would have liked to do more than that little bow, but in his condition no larger movement or statement could be expected of him. To cling to her, gawky and speaking thickly: he was able, in spite of being so intoxicated, to keep himself from doing this. And yet her heart is beating harder after this encounter and the sight of this man, so near to her and so far. A little later she hears a waitress in the background, upset and shouting so loudly that the whole restaurant looks up.

'Heavens, Herr Bekker, Herr Bekker! . . . You've wet yourself . . . wet through! Well!—aren't you ashamed of yourself?' The people snigger at their tables. The waitress enjoys getting into scenes with drunks, in order to expose them in the stupidest of ways before an audience, and the people are used to it. She bellows at Grit's father as you would to a slow child or the village idiot. He needs some time before he succeeds in breaking through his muteness—as if it were an inner sound barrier. First of all, though his mouth is wide open, nothing comes. Then a very profound and fundamental groan, such as you hear from time to time from sleepy dogs, so like a human sound that you imagine the creature must next begin to speak as well. At last he says, with heavy emphasis: 'Oh, where?' And the waitress, the serving-woman carrying her fully laden tray of beers, goes on with her coarse scene in front of all the guests: 'There! Just look at your fly . . . wet through, Herr Bekker.' Everyone in the inn, including those who can't see anything, now guffaws loudly, though some of them, admittedly amused, remind the waitress to behave with greater decency. Grit has not turned round; she sits motionless at her table. 'Just you hang on,' cries the waitress, 'I'll bring you something to mop up with.' Then she runs hastily on and serves the beers.

Suddenly her father is sitting beside Grit on the seat. He has fled the stage and its ordeals, has fled his buddies and mockers. Grit looks at him sideways. He is sitting very close to her. He endeavours to cross his legs under the table and at the same time to prop up his right arm so as to dig about in a gap in his teeth with his thumbnail. Again he seeks refuge in an inconspicuous and occupied demeanour which might give form to his fear, his chaos, his lack of strength or speech. But his elbow slips from the table-edge again and again, and his right leg cannot surmount his left knee. At last he leans back, lets his arms drop where they will, stretches out and sinks his chin on to his chest. Now Grit notices that it was not without cause that the waitress poked fun at her father. His fly is half open and around it the grey material is stained dark and moist. Now, with him lying beside her with his legs apart, there is an acrid smell of urine.

[49]

As long as he doesn't chafe himself sore! thinks Grit quite involuntarily, and blushes at this misplaced moment of motherly concern. She beckons her waitress, the one that appropriates other people's facial expressions, and has her tot up the bill. For both of them. Yes, now look over here, all of you, and see we're together . . .

'I cannot put it into words,' her father often says nowadays, quietly bemused when he tries to reminisce and suddenly breaks off. He thinks and speaks and gives up in the middle of his sentence. 'That's not the way it was.' He remembers badly. For Grit, this whole manner of her father's which he has been revealing recently is difficult to understand. He seems to her alternately alert and dull, desirous and fatigued, clever and ignorant. An educated person, still strong and physically healthy too, who is beset by age in his best years, as if by an insidious disease. And yet it is especially when recounting things from the past that he gets stuck—which is otherwise the favourite pastime of elderly people, particularly when they have their children with them. One thing is certain: that he is doing himself damage, his brain too, with too much alcohol, too much cognac. She feels she must take steps against this misuse more rigorously than before, must more relentlessly use the means at her disposal, and at the same time she believes that nonetheless something else, something more mysterious, could be helping to bring about this deformation of his mature years of manhood. In all seriousness she has resolved to look up Ageing, Sudden, in medical handbooks as soon as she can. She also thinks she can recall a film or an old story, something well-known, in which a particular poison or magical fruit played a part, and those who partook of it did not die on the spot but instantly began to age, the years passing at a faster rate, body and mind disintegrating unstoppably. And at times she now thinks: he's just taking life easy. He has simply resigned to laziness, has locked himself away from his enemy and his few friends, and now laziness will no longer release him. It is corroding the whole man, his will, his heart, his language, his muscles. A do-nothing reaches his furthest frontiers. Then again, she only need look into his reddened, fearful eyes which gaze up from the depths of indolence to recognize that he no longer has any choice and he has become the victim of an inoculated hasty decay which he can no longer hold up by exertion of his own powers. His eyes can just about still say it clearly: Look here, what an incomprehensible thing is happening to me! while his mouth can already no longer say it clearly. His speech goes awry, he stammers, mixes up stupidity and old-time adages that no one understands any more nowadays. In all this, the tortured one nonetheless always seems well-rested. He sleeps long, drinks in full draughts, goes to patisseries. Every day Bekker and Grit take a longish excursion by car and on foot. Grit does the planning and sees to it that the programmes are kept to and not too much dead time is left over. Only recently, the drive to the Dachstein was impressive: to the Gosausee, which has been dammed, and from here the ascent on foot to the Hinterer Gosausee. A lonely walk that leads you into the silence and cold of the upper mountain world, along stony paths that lie covered with thin frozen-over snow, and all the time through damp, black forest which, however peacefully and in-differently it stands there, is yet too familiar and too ill-famed from fairy tales and bad dreams not to depress you, and through which by the end they had once again gone wandering astray, abandoned and unnatural, just like Hänsel and Gretel.

You do not see the smaller lake gradually while walking to it, you see it suddenly, gleaming darkly ahead of you. On its opposite bank there is a little house to which no visible path leads down. Behind the hut the pines rise on the hillside. In the snow, down to the lakeside, there are no footprints. When there is snow on the ground all sound in the mountains is as blunt and dry as in a recording studio. Something or other crackles softly in the distance. Whereupon the door of the hut opposite opens and a lean man in grey fatigues steps out. He waves at the walkers . . . like an explosives expert or a soldier:

do not walk any further, and do not look this way any more!

Immediately they obey the instruction and turn round without hesitating and without thinking about the man any more. Along the way the daughter takes hold of her father's sleeve once and they remain standing. 'I'd like to ask you something,' she says, 'why don't you have a woman friend, and no real friend? Try for once to answer.'

Her father murmurs something incomprehensible and rushes three paces forward, as if a large dog had pulled him by the lead.

'It seems to me you must go back to the Institute soon, and if they don't want you go somewhere else, among men. They're what you need, you see. It was like that before as well. Now you seem older than you are a lot of the time. Sometimes you don't even talk quite right. And you drink too much . . .'

'Och, I'm not really old,' replies her father absently and comfortably, 'and I don't particularly live in my memories.' As he now goes on, in silence, he senses how much he misses the city and the peace the city grants him now and then. The way you finally sit down on a bench in the early morning after a night of walking, out there in an empty playground in the outskirts of some commuter town. The broad stone block of a tenement building in the cool morning. At twenty-past six the lights flash on in the little kitchens from top to bottom, criss-cross, right the way over the whole wall. Workingman with wife in dressing gown and a thermos flask on the table. Workingman with wife, both dressed for work, at the kitchen table. Wife alone in jeans and pullover with a coffee cup, standing. One morning in more than fifty little windows, as on a honeycomb of video screens . . .

On the one hand there's money, which we earn plenty of (even I do, still, with the worst humiliations, I get it from a guaranteed source), on the other Germany, whose scraping and pushing we cannot accurately assess and observe however attentively we stare and prick up our ears, we inadequate diviners of contemporary events. There we sit next to it all, well-to-do, in our soundproof booth, dry, and sounds we make ourselves die away feebly beside us. The time has long come for rebellion behind the glass. Sooner or later we will have to leap through the soundproof pane. . . . For ages I have seen no one who can look straight. I only see them forking their food into them and straining their brains and thinking out witticisms, well-schooled remarks about things never seen. Women pass by, without feeling even the slightest sense of quest. Their faces are sealed off either by aimless self-assertion or by nameless horror. Thus they have long since become sisters of the *status quo*, the dismal residue of endeavour that has ceased to glow, and never again will they see a promise of better things to come. . . . And yet, when you have spent your hope on the whole horizon, only one place remains, one place in the world that's worthy of all longing, no house on the heath, no garden however fine, nor freedom either, but simply the Completely Different Way of Seeing. To be looked at just once in such a way as to dissolve all remnants of dirt from the soul. Just once the good, the civilizing look that would fill a little inner courtyard with peace! Oh, but you really have to take a good look at each other, patiently immerse yourselves in each other's eyes, to gain the certainty that you really don't need to be afraid of each other. One mere jab of the eyes or a miserable glance is not enough—it only increases the world's evil rays!—nor eyes that listen to your own words without restraint . . . Love awaits the light of the eyes. When the light of the eyes shines, you're happy. And we can slap wet belly against wet belly as often as we like, our bodies can thrash about or we can flounder like musk-rats, we never come any closer to the crux of the matter than with our eyes, which cannot be united. . . . 'Look into the sun, my lad,' the officer often said during his last days, 'look into the sun with your eyes open, it strengthens the eye. The sun does everything, it alone does everything. That we can see at all and the earth is colourful is the sun's doing alone.' After lunch his armchair was shifted to the open window where he would have the sun love him, couldn't get enough. He—who hated everything that moves—visibly took a lustful pleasure in the sun.

[53]

Grit looks at her father, walking beside her with his head bowed. This man, who gushes a frightful torrent of words one day and then the next doesn't open his mouth at all any more. This man, who after all could answer all her questions once upon a time and knew so much. Now the educator has grown uncertain. The child leads a stammerer about the country, whom you can no longer ask about anything. If the worst came to the worst he could not even give her the slightest scrap of sensible advice. He would educate her higgledy-piggledy into a state of confusion and error if she were still small now and needed his help!

After the evening meal they sit in their rooms, each at a little table, wall to wall. Grit means to spend four weeks at the Mondsee but then celebrate Christmas at home. Four weeks in this wet darkness? Well, it is her only holiday in the year, so four weeks it is to be. How to get through them? The abundance and the pressure of hours to come at times force Bekker into a time-squeeze that chokes up his chest. The delay is colossal. He sits at his little table and Zachler is so far. From time to time he puts an ear to the wall and listens to Grit going to bed. Conditions of paralysis or of panic are not least the result of his harrowing efforts to limit his drinking, to change from cognac to wine, to small amounts of wine, of light wine. For recently he and Grit had a clamorous row, as suddenly as crows flapping up.

'But you can't treat me like an idiot my whole life long, just because you once saw me drunk!'

'Once? Often!'

'Never properly drunk.'

'No? What then? If you're crawling on all fours and can no longer say boo?'

'I see it all, I see it all. . . . It's senseless scolding the seer.'

'The what—?'

And so on. A violent racket that passed over as quickly as it arose. But nonetheless it has turned Grit in on herself and left her in restless despondency. Involuntarily she feels reminded of the terrible quarrels between her parents.

After a last deep insult with which her mother finally puts a snarling end to the mean exchange of words at supper, her father leaves their table and locks himself in his room. Not even the child, later sent to effect a reconciliation, is allowed in. It is not until shortly before midnight that he comes out again, dressed to go out, and briefly tells her mother that he intends to go for a walk, to be exact along the path to the waterworks that leads, as we know, across a certain bridge, along a certain railway embankment. The time of his return is shrouded in mystery. The little girl stands there howling pitifully at her father, who looks at her so cruelly as if it were the last time.

When towards morning he inserts the key in the lock and the bridge and the track have again released him, Grit jumps from her bed and runs to him, clings to his hip, hangs on to the pockets of his coat. Then he takes the little one on to his arm and they both laugh with relief. He takes her back to her room and rocks her to the rhymes of 'Wie war zu Köln es doch vordem' and, when they get to 'Denn, war man faul, man legte sich hin auf das Bett und pflegte sich', drops her from his swinging hands into the soft castle of pillows. Grit squeaks and kicks, ruffles her father's hair and pulls him by the ear-lobes to her face and kisses him on the mouth.

Once in later years, when Grit is already going to high school, not long before the first trip to the Mondsee, and Bekker only occasionally comes to visit, he surreptitiously watches his child at a sensitive age in which each additional hour, almost indeed each moment, might tip the scales into womanhood. The lips gently arched up, but her nose still turned-up and dainty, her eyes already inquisitively opened, gazing with a peculiar brevity but also accuracy in that way that only mistrusting, active people have. (By the by, this was lost later. It was no doubt a part of that impatience with which, in those

[55]

days, she couldn't bear waiting for her own becoming and finally being finished.) The way she pushes back her hair from her brow with the back of her hand, pricks her fork into her meat: all this is still awkward and immature. And yet, through affectation and manners, forms are already rounded out that need only a little more practice and finesse to be fully developed and no longer attract attention. Nay, perhaps all that is still lacking is the one decisive moment, and afterwards immaturity is forever gone. Her father would not care to be guilty of this. He hardly dares take Grit's arm any more, even hesitates to speak candidly to her or to irritate her somehow, always afraid he could unfavourably influence her unsettled vision with all this, and something premature, ahead of its hour, maturity itself would suddenly break out, just at that moment when she would have to respond to him . . .

No, this is not a memory. The way he looks at her today he cannot at all remember how she once was as a child. It is not memory, this aimless erection on seeing her cast-off clothing. This explodes memory: completely domestic recollection will now have to be blown sky-high. . . . If at times she permits him to remain sitting with her in her room in the evening while she reads, the tears start to his eyes for very well-wishing and well-being. He has a craving for harmony with his child. Now and then when he is going under, or stammering, or when his vision has gone pitch black, he grabs her hand and holds tight. And she allows him to do so, rather less than allows him. It is not likely that she could feel anything other than patience for him. Nor is it likely that she feels very much at all, in general. Her whole soul is a confined circuit, and she is a little too self-sufficient. Never commanded to resist, born to accept and get along, her very being lacks, as do so many of her contemporaries, the pulsation of the fight and of intolerance. Indeed, it looks as if time has made the very opposite of patricides of our children. Father and son, with colourful, thick-knotted ties, specially chosen for colour TV, sit next to each other in the quiz boxes and between them know all there is to know about Elvis, his life, his songs, his films, his shows. They belong to the same fan club too, the forty-year-old and the sixty-year-old alike. They do not argue; they complement each other, united in the cult of the selfsame idol. Together they know simply everything about Elvis. They possess a unique collection, a precious archive with countless newspaper clippings, photos, autographs given or purchased, and during the broadcast they show in a transparent *bonbonnière* a white silk cloth that Elvis used during his last performance to dab the sweat from his brow. Every other year they travel to Memphis in their holidays, and in front of Graceland, the singer's property, they unfurl large banners on which the greetings and best wishes of their club have been painted. Even after his death—which 'in principle' they don't believe in—they have been over there yet again. What they do believe in is the existence of dozens of cameras, movie cameras concealed everywhere in the walls of Graceland, by means of which He in his bedroom can see all his fans before the gates on numerous video screens, while He lies on his bed and drinks one Coke after another—He sees us all! . . . The father, a drilling technician from Bakum in the administrative district of Vechta, says: 'I like Elvis because for me he embodies purity.' His son says: 'He has given other people so much strength. When you listen to him you never lose faith in yourself.'

Grit reads a book at the Mondsee that she can't really take to and whose pages she occasionally flips forward impatiently. Joseph gave it her to take along: *The Barque* by Louis Malomy. The hero of the novel, always merely labelled M., has invited a small bevy of friends and those closest to him aboard his yacht, to flee New York and all civilization, like Noah in his Ark. The fiasco of this voyage is pictured crudely and longwindedly. At the end a totally wrecked community of completely delirious individuals returns on a veritable ship of death to the home

[57]

port. 'But who is this M. in the novel?' asks Grit, and promptly replies to her complete satisfaction: 'But that's Malomy himself, of course. M. equals Malomy.' 'Not necessarily,' says Bekker eagerly, 'it's not usually so simple. If it were, Malomy could just say I. But even if he said I it would by no means be certain that he, Malomy, the author, is also the hero of the novel. That's how it is with a good many novels.' Though in this her father has at long last given a reply with some thought content, such as Grit is after, she does not follow him but looks back disappointed at her book. 'I don't understand that.' And in saying this she seems to think: what a pointless puzzle! That only makes the business more complicated.

How beautiful, how deep and stupid, with soft relaxed cheeks, this pensive woman looks when she is reading, feeling slightly offended, her head bent over her book which lies in her lap. He is taken with feelings of tenderness for this unskilled reader. How willingly he would be prepared, and how able, to follow her into her limitedness and parrot all her nonsense. How cosily you could be accommodated in these restricted views, in these safe and false convictions!

She reads several pages, without stopping. Then, suddenly, a deep sigh: 'So true! So true!' she exclaims and snaps the book shut. As if she meant to say: once it begins to be that true I don't need a book any more. Her cheeks are full, with no sunken hollows, and quickly take on a glow. (Is that perhaps the way in? Perhaps that is the first glow coming through from the lowest circle of hell to which I must descend? Nowadays you no longer know where the entrance is actually concealed . . .)

Once more an outing to Salzburg. Along the walls, head bowed. Walking in the city again, at last. The mossy darkness of all the narrow streets, now in the early winter, the sky perpetually clouded over, embeds you, but at an unearthly place, near the abyss. Grit is suddenly and without reason overcome by abject misery. But she walks bravely and hastily beside her father. And these very paces, taken briskly together, this feeling that she makes up some vague, strong pair with her father, seems quite simply to shake out the tears above. They are still flowing undiminished when in the late afternoon in the Tomaselli she develops an unnatural appetite and wolfs a massive quantity of food, in order, as it appears, to fill up an emptiness and longing created by very existence. Bekker looks on in blank amazement to see how emotion and gobbling greed can so well coexist. One after the other Grit eats up a sirloin steak, a salad, two cheese sandwiches, one with Camembert, one with Edam, and to finish a piece of punch gateau and one of Sachertorte.

After this has all been polished off her cheeks glow again, her weeping is over. She looks up into her father's face from her empty plate with a guilty beauty. The corners of her mouth, pulled down, sketch an expression of contempt. But then her mouth opens and she smiles brightly. And yet just past him. She is smiling at someone else, a man behind his back who is sitting alone at his table, a dark-skinned foreigner, by the look of him an Indian, elegantly dressed, his shirt and suit in matt shades of grey that tone down and soften the intense black of his head. All of a sudden Grit stretches and embraces her father, snuggles up to him violently. Thus unexpectedly drawn to her breast in his crouched-up position and uncomfortably squeezed, he hesitantly places his hands on her back, self-consciously strokes her between the shoulders, but then slowly downward as well.

He thinks, instead of nothing he thinks: oh, I know very well what her face is doing up there now . . . There across my shoulder it is signalling to the Indian. And I know what it is saying, too. See, it says, this is what it's like when I hold someone in my arms and squeeze him tight. It can be very good, believe me. And if you like it, you can give it a try too . . . 'Helphelp,' she is just whispering above his ear. Helphelp does not indeed really mean anything, it merely escapes her, just like that, as a sigh of pleasure, as other people say 'terrific'

or 'fantastic' if they are satisfied or astonished. Bekker pushes
her gently back into her seat now. When they are once again
vis-à-vis he puts his hand on the table, index finger raised, to
give the sign for a more serious explanation. But nowadays
Grit cannot take seriously that threatening finger that used to
be raised to the fidgety child; she seizes it in her little fist and
strokes the tip with her thumb. The Indian cannot miss this!
'What's up?' she asks, her lips wry, and lecherous crinkles
appear under her eyes. Bekker reddens and shudders. What the
hell, I'm just a dummy for the Indian, he thinks, just a doll to
use as an example, which she uses to show off her seductive
holds. Now she starts to play the whispering seductress, in
sweet tones and with many turns of the head she pours out the
most untruthful confessions. How fortunate, though, that her
father has come close to her once more in life: for ten years they
took no notice of each other, ten years of indifference, but now
at last, alone with him now, for the first time ever a feeling like
this for her father, a human being she would once more like to
ask about everything, whom she'd like to look after, care for,
leave off her wrong relationships and only obey. . . . She
slides to and fro on her chair, more and more restless, hugs her
father anew and suddenly from mid-hug leaps to her feet as
this gruesome exercise in gush has reached its climax with a
renewed 'Helphelp!', jumps up from the table, tosses her long
hair from her shoulders so that the Indian should be made
familiar with this too, and then disappears in the direction of
the toilets . . .

    They're shooting over me. The brat! Shots are fired, I am
near to the source of the shooting but I do not know where it is
coming from. . . . Like when you ride home in summer from
bathing in the lake, five o'clock on a hot afternoon, and you
pass the school hostel, where a girls' choir is practising old
German songs. Then the shots ring out. Your girlfriend
behind you and her bike slam down with a clatter on the
country lane. Above you the shooting continues, the choir
breaks off, bent double you race across the grass to the hostel,
vault in at the open window and hide among the choir of girls,

who crowd in close above you. From your chattering mouth you slobber on to the jeans of one of these womanly children, small hands with varnished finger-nails holding you down by the back of your head. These wise and courageous girls protect and hide out. But she with whom you just now took a dip in the water is lying out there on the road, shot dead. Who did it? Some authority? Some gunman firing at random? Who was she in any case? Now she is lying there, dead, her eyes wide open, in contorted peace. No word can touch that any more. That, the dead woman, is a thing, so much a thing that no language, not even her own name, can name it any more. Nowhere does any blood flow from her. Only her eyes are two fat, bloody little bags. Not a single drop of blood comes from her. It collects in her eyes and distends them and bends them out . . .

The child touched me! And it is as if this one touch had been enough to break my rigid stiffness and melt down everything into the undifferentiated mass of wishes and desires once more.

She has been away a long time. Too long for small business. From all round the coffee-house people glance at me, glance across while turning the page of a newspaper or glance up from a tête-a-tête. Everyone knows, after all, that the little one who was just being so nice to me is now dumping a big heap of shit. I must look correspondingly abandoned. No wonder if you're driven to destroying napkins and kneading bread-crumbs. Like a detective on the trail of the last promising clue I try to recall everything she said to me, to restore it word for word. I recite it to myself once again silently, repeat it in a whisper, test the echoes to see if there isn't somewhere a sound, a little word, a breath, that could unambiguously indicate more, a little hint that was not solely intended for the Indian to look at. But all the indications that I examine more closely, even those favourable to me, in the last analysis remain doubtful, alternating unbearably between promise and deceit. 'Now we are alone . . .' A statement threatening death or a statement of the fullest accommodation. Suction, fear, warmth, senses put out of joint by primaeval beginnings as soon as—in the very first betrothal of looks, gloomily and with rattling chains—love's torture machine starts running and the door of the concentration chamber is barred up from outside. Alone with your own child . . . banished and gone to ruin, locked away in a heavenly dungeon, powerless, utterly powerless, to resist solely by the pure force of one muscle, for there is only One Muscle and nothing else between her and me. Here, at the end of the endless event, at the end of reproduction and species, there remain only growth and increase, going beyond the devouring the self. Total disappearance. The highest consecration of purposeless love and the celebration of its contra-social nature, incest. And there is nothing of playing in it, no dreams any longer, no irony, even if the familiar grin of lust stays fixed on our lips to the very end . . .

Grit returns. No. It is senseless. Hardly do I see her but the intoxication comes to a stop. The one No. Nothing remains for me, nothing, but to crouch modestly in my corner and masturbate to her health. I am only afraid of growing older still. And of becoming mulish. Just able to know old age before you are it. Completely mulish . . .

In contrast to when she went, her pace is now without buoyancy or any energy at all. She comes almost creeping, bowed and slow. Some people look down at her feet. One of the heels of her boots has transfixed a strip of toilet paper from the floor and now she drags it along behind her without noticing. She smiles slightly at the Indian, now frankly if also wearily saying no. Such a good natured and everyday smirk appears on the foreign face when it discovers the unworthy tail she is pulling along that everything secret, the very darkness vanishes from it. Grit sits down again at the table, rests her brow in her hand. Her cheeks are blotched with red, little drops of sweat stand on the white tip of her nose. She complains of terrible pains in her abdomen. For whole minutes she was unable to move, she says. She looks at her father earnestly and distractedly, as if she were hearkening to the fading tumult of the pain. All of a sudden she is very, very alone and transposed into the sober, pale world of worry. She who was just chock-full of suggestive charm and tomfoolery. Softly she asks if they can pay and also asks her father to drive her home so that she does not have to sit at the wheel herself. When they go out, as he is helping her into her parka, Bekker tries carefully to step on the paper which is still trailing from her heel. Whereupon she notices it, turns and looks quite without interest at the torn strip without being even remotely embarrassed. Only one last dull look across at the Indian seems to say: there you are, something ridiculous left over from me, lying there—just consider it the torn, spattered flag that always flutters at the end of desire, however it goes . . .

Bekker drives Grit's car for the first time, the green Peugeot whose brakes need attention, and drives it carefully along the freeway to the Mondsee. Grit lies on the back seat with her legs pulled up, a blanket wrapped about her hips. She stares motionless at the grain of the imitation leather upholstery and lies in wait for the swelling and diminishing of the pressure in abdomen. She has never yet known complaints of this intensity. Reluctantly, and only in response to persistent questioning by her father, she tells of her illness and acts as if she really had nothing to do with it. 'It's a perpetual inflammation,' she says, 'caused by this quantity of residual urine I retain, and that in turn is because something is wrong with my spinal cord at the bottom.' Her father criticizes her close-mouthed information, which makes no connection apparent between the origin and effects of her illness. Gradually it turns out that she has already been getting treatment for a long time on account of a bladder ailment. Last summer she submitted to a first neurological examination after her urologist had stuffed her, nay, regularly pumped her (as they say in drug parlance) full of antibiotics for years, without ever trying to get at the causes of her com-

[63]

plaints. In the clinic, at last, they took a myelogram, an X-ray of her spinal cord. To inject the contrast fluid the assistant medic needed to puncture the spinal canal, and in doing so must presumably have hit the root of a nerve; at all events, a hellish pain flashed through her leg. Afterwards she felt so awful and so weakened by the fractional loss of cerebro-spinal fluid usual with such a puncture that she had to rest for a whole week in a hospital bed. Scared off by the strain that this preliminary examination alone had put her through, she then dug in her heels against any further treatment at that clinic. She rejected neurosurgery, which the doctors nonetheless urged her to undergo, since the result of the myelography had shown rather suspect findings: thickenings like little bags, bulbous distensions, had been discovered at the lower end of the spinal cord. These, they said, could be responsible for any kind of disturbances in the region of the pelvis, insofar as they exerted direct pressure on those nerve fibres which control the sphincter vesicae, among other things. To find out more exactly what was wrong they would have only one option: to open her up, to cut her open. That was what the doctor told her. But Grit did not want to have herself cut open, least of all right away and in summer. And besides, she was afraid of a graver certainty. The doctors had admittedly not cared, in their own words, to rule out the suspicion of a tumour, but had made the reservation that a malignant growth was most particularly uncommon in this region, the 'pony-tail' of the spinal cord. True, her even stronger fear was that during the operation, which demands the most fiddly dexterity, another slip might happen, a nerve would be injured or severed, and she would come round from the anaesthetic a cripple. That such a danger existed, albeit only in the eventuality of a total removal of the growths being undertaken (which the surgeon conducting the operation would, however, only be able to decide on the spot): this they had in fact cautiously made known to her. Immediately she refused to give her consent to the operation. Rather, she decided to let the illness stay as it had been till then and to go on living as she hitherto had done with

[64]

her complaints, which she had half grown accustomed to. In this idle and foolish attitude she is strongly confirmed by her mother, who (always only on the phone, from Southern Germany) gives her any amount of superstitious advice and, of course, has just experienced the very same case among her closest acquaintances, a woman of Grit's age, confined to a wheelchair for ever after the operation. Just don't let them open you up, child! Margarete, you see, refuses categorically to have any operation whatsoever done on the complete whole of the human body. Instead she swears by yoga, macrobiotic food and strict homeopathy. Bekker attempts to make the general dangers and the craziness of such an attitude clear to his daughter, particularly if unambiguous evidence of physical illness is at hand. To this the only response he gets is that there is no such thing in the body as something unambiguously physical. Confronted with so much benighted recklessness and faith–healing, the rational man in him, the scientific thinker, comes to the fore with quite unexpected vehemence. He becomes more and more worked-up and sober and preaches the logic of illness and medicine, using the most appropriate terms and cleverest examples, his work at the Institute having trained him in familiarizing himself quickly and approximately with the most disparate technical languages and communicative systems. Nor does this obstinate holding–forth fail to have its effect on Grit. She even regains her own interest in her illness. He is really concerned, she thinks, how nice of him. And on top of that she is pleased that in the process he is gradually emerging from his misty domains and becoming a quite unintoxicated man whom you might after all be able to rely on if once things got serious and danger threatened.

In the pension she requests him to accompany her to her room for a short while. There she rapidly and without embarrassment undresses in front of his eyes, uncovers the lower half of her body as if she were at the doctor's, stands up straight, her legs close together, and observes how quickly he grasps what cannot be missed: the left leg is somewhat thinner than the right about the calf, perhaps four or five centimetres in circumference. It is noticeable. 'The calf is numb,' she says, and takes hold of it. She feels nothing there. The muscles have gone limp. This signifies no more than that sometimes when she walks she cannot feel her left foot any more at all. Then she thinks she will fall over instantly. But she doesn't. Mutely, Bekker gapes at the all too suddenly and painfully aired secret, the hip, the lower nakedness that is, however, bound in tighter by concern and clinical bareness than by a chastity belt. Stiff and graceless she stands there nude, an express punishment of anyone who had ever dared to imagine her naked. Bekker feels profoundly a moment of the knife and of penitence: the delirious phallus beheaded and robbed of its profligate fantasies. The gaze of the uprooted father and dazzled voyeur only slowly recovers, and gains the necessary cool, calm attention to those parts of the body alone which Grit is actually showing him and which are critical. And yet he is the same man who just now, in the safety of her unattainability, dreamed of this nakedness, and if her hips and pubic hair had now, too, appeared to him with the quality of a dream, he would have felt nothing other than a momentary reversion to primitive wildness and the shadowing of the whole earth by one female giant torso in the firmament. As it is, the sidelong leer remains and a slight catching of the breath, nothing is wholly cancelled out. Grit turns around and points to two dark patches on her behind. 'Dead spots,' she says, and tries to look down at them across her shoulder. 'The tissue there is no longer supplied with blood. Numb too.' The curve of her body, clothed to the hip, the narrow backside turned to the fore—this pin-up image of the cheapest kind and, countering it, the bitter symptoms: the dead patches, the withered leg, residual urine, paralysis of the sphincter vesicae, an inflamed renal pelvis . . . 'Now I'll show you something else,' she says, and stretches out her left foot. 'You see? A claw foot. Practically crippled. That's probably a result of the trapped nerves in my spinal cord as well. Basically all I've shown you is one single problem. And I've always had the claw foot. Even

[66]

as a little girl. Why ever did you never see it? You didn't and Margarete didn't either. Did you ever really look at me properly? If a claw foot crops up you always have to consider what causes it. It's usually the spine . . . the spinal cord. But you noticed nothing and I always supposed it was the ballet lessons that did it—a high instep is nothing unusual in ballet. Helphelp. I mean, look, you check your child over to see if it's okay. Parents know better than the child what is straight and what's crooked.' Meanwhile she has pulled on a pair of tights and has firmly wrapped the blanket, which she brought with her from the car, about her abdomen. Like this she goes to bed, swallows two tablets of her medicine with her eyes screwed up, and then adds: 'For ten years or even longer, or ever since my birth, something's been going wrong. That's also why it's unlikely to be cancer, these things in my back. There's a good side to it too.' Whereupon she contemplates her father in a somewhat strange and averse manner, sees how he does nothing but stand heavily in the room, his hands in the pockets of his jacket, only breathes louder and does not go.

She wishes him good-night, her inflexion intimating that she would like him to leave her alone now. He remains standing a while longer, as if he were searching for an attitude, a response. But the serious and sudden revelations Grit has made concerning her illness are still buzzing too newly in his head. Beneath the burden of the last few moments, shifting from desire to concern, he cannot utter a syllable, remains awkwardly silent. He merely echoes her good-night softly and then goes slowly to the next room.

Grit's complaints continue. After a slight improvement during the following few days, when they are at least still able to make a shorter outing or so, it all ends in one terrible night when the pains in her abdomen well-nigh rob her of breath and consciousness, and can no longer be alleviated by medicine. She feels as if the build-up of urine were blowing up her bladder like a balloon and nearly causing it to burst. When she does not appear at breakfast in the morning Bekker runs up to her room and finds her pale and flat out on her pillow, distraught and exhausted, with an impression of terror and nothingness on her round face. She barely dares to make even the slightest movement any more, and looks into his eyes with effort from a distance to which torment and mortal danger have removed her, mutely hunting for help or meaning, so that once again he must feel ashamed on account of his silence and his incompetent sympathy. A doctor is summoned from the village, although Grit thinks it useless and still believes her condition will improve of its own accord. A youngish man appears a short time later, dressed with a curious elegance for a country doctor (with a pearl tie-pin, like a bourgeois gentleman of times gone by!), and on top of it he is a Hungarian, speaking that selfsame lazy-lipped German that always makes you think of operettas and which drives you to despair in serious situations. All the more rigorous is the content of his instructions. He does not consider it possible to see Grit painlessly through her holiday with medicines and injections. She must go into hospital immediately: there is no alternative. Grit takes a look at the Hungarian to check whether he isn't overdoing it. When someone speaks this kind of German you're reluctant to believe anything. But his eyes are clear, so steady and experienced, although he is not old in years. So no doubt he is right . . . 'Manstett,' says Grit feebly, but not too feebly to twist her mouth contemptuously down as she forms the name. Manstett, the neuro-surgeon back home at the west end clinic; Manstett, the chief, who would have wanted to open her up long ago and assured her that a bed was always ready for her and she only needed to call if her condition suddenly deteriorated. Grit consults with her father as to the next necessary steps. The Mondsee vacation must be broken off—or rather, interrupted, as she immediately corrects herself when her father nods too eagerly. They can return home with the least trouble if they fly from Salzburg. The Peugeot can be collected later or they can even have it driven up, just depending. After this night and this upsurge of pain Grit is ready, helplessly willing to have them open her up.

Manstett is rated number one in his field—Grit has found out—beyond the city too, even beyond Germany itself. He must be in his mid-fifties, a lean personage, and his arms are over-long like a chimpanzee's—which has a disturbing effect in one who has to do precision work with his hands—while his shoulders are scrawny and narrow. A festoon of auburn curls lies about his bald skull, which, like the white, thin skin of his face, is speckled with freckles. He looks ill, looks it both naturally and hereditarily, as a bad diabetic might look. An ill, obsessed surgeon, you think, a sombre expert, perhaps even a devil in the service of health. Grit consulted him once again and Manstett succeeded, if not in dispelling her fear of the impending operation, at least in subduing it to a large degree. He treated her as if she were his honoured partner in the performance of his operation—like a conductor who with great composure reaches an agreement with the pianist about an oft-played concerto—although she will lie before him no more than an unconscious piece of meat the next morning.

So she moves into room 18 in Ward B with a small suitcase that contains the clothes she had not yet used on the holiday. At the same time Bekker again takes a room in the little hotel where he lived when he returned from Oldenburg and was still roaming all day long through the city before plucking up the courage to phone his daughter and appear before her. It is situated almost opposite the hospital. From his fourth-floor room he can see the façade of the north wing, the balconies where the patients from the rooms with several beds step out in dressing-gowns to smoke. In these days before Christmas it has suddenly turned bewilderingly mild, almost as warm as in spring, and the crocuses are already flowering in the hospital garden.

This evening Bekker lies fully dressed on his bed. He has not been drinking, he does not want to go out. Drowsily he listens to the wind passing through the prematurely mild night, and it takes the form of a kindly arm reaching out across the land, rattling in the capstan-like trees, slowly rises to him, stirs at his open window, and just a mere breath of it, as if from the wave of a hand, enters the room and brushes his brow with its fingertips. That was the mighty arm, and it is gone. At half-past eight tomorrow morning Grit will be opened up. . . . In his half-dozing state, feelings of guilt foment, he is aghast at his omission of so many, many years ago—'I didn't look at her foot!'—just as, in a dream, you experience the last second before an inevitable accident in full consciousness. . . . An unfavourably placed traffic sign, hidden by delicate fresh leafage, the very last absolute STOP sign that has anyone who fails to see it racing to his destruction. . . Stop, Grit! Don't let them cut you open! Come out before it's too late, before the anaesthetic! Fear and superstition have taken hold of him now, he recants all the rationality of the day, of when he was awake. Suddenly he hears himself repeating in court words he spoke to his child, or could have spoken, or else he hears the magistrate ask them: 'Thereupon you are said to have told the plaintiff that you would not be the least bit alarmed if, when you saw her again, she was confined to a wheelchair. On the contrary, you, the accused, derived a certain satisfaction from the thought that the plaintiff would, in the eventuality of her being totally helpless, be completely dependent on your care and support . . .' Bekker's leg twitches, while in his dream he yells and protests, and still all he does is kick in vain against the aluminium lid of the coffin of sleep, he does not wake, and the dream of damnation goes on, this dream in which one unavoidable evil after the other has forever to be averted. . . . It is as if you had to chase after a letter you've mailed, from post office to post office, catch up with it yourself, a letter to your own mother, say, containing annihilating abuse, words that stop the heartbeat like secret microwaves, a general reckoning drawn up one evening after a whole day's failed labour, blaming her for every one of these never-ending failures, without reason, comprehensively, and you've mailed this long, dangerous letter late at night in the collection box at the station and afterwards you've announced it's on its way with your hand brandished threateningly aloft and then you've fallen into a leaden sleep from which next morning you awake with flashes of remorse and immediately chase after the letter, you try to catch up with it personally, you feelingly and cleverly work on the officials who supervise the sorting equipment, you shirk no revelation, but only to discover that the letter has probably already left town at six that morning, so now without hesitating you leave town too, as according to one official's assurances despatches to southernmost Germany take a full day, now you sit for light years in the express train, almost losing the object of all your actions from view, and then nonetheless you get down in Füssen and, ducking, run to the little garden at your mother's house, just don't let her see you, rather spend a night freezing in the bushes, till the following morning the postman arrives, and, straightening up from deep contemplation of the tulip bed, you greet him and approach him as if you were one of the household and have him give you the post, where along with the lottery ticket and notification from the health insurance there is indeed that criminal letter, you take it and push the rest carefully into the house through the slit in the door, but then shortly after you see your mother coming out and at the sight of her, on seeing her hateful little hat and hearing her hateful little small talk that she gushes forth while gassing to the woman next door, you find that that very *profundis* of the soul is shown to be true, from the depths of which you wrote the letter and blamed all your daily failure on your mother, on her and the endlessly fruitful echo of her empty words in your ears, that never-to-be-eradicated moment of her first disheartened look at your tiny, still wet brow . . .

'On the day of the operation we cannot allow any visitors to see patients', the matron says, and tips a bag of biscuits on to a paper plate. Bekker remains undecided in front of the glass pane of the matron's room. It does not look as if he could beg special permission from this brusque old miss. Two Korean women are sitting at a table on which a small Christmas-tree

[71]

has been stood; they stretch out their short legs to each other and tap each other with the tips of their shoes. There is a smell of potato soup and surgical dressing. The patient is as well as you would expect under the circumstances. She is asleep. One of the two owl-headed girls blethers incessantly, addressing the matron's back; her gob goes on like a chaff-cutter, shaking our Good German about and hacking it into pieces and scattering it in a thousand unrecognizable scraps around the place. This goes on with neither a pause nor any inhibition, helter-skelter, one single turbulent complaint—this much can just about be understood—about the intolerable difficulties involved in finding a flat for herself and this friend to share.

In the corridor patients are lying in wheeled beds, waiting to be transported to their X-ray examinations in the basement. Two male nurses come along, one in a particularly expansive mood, bellowing so sonorously when he greets an old woman that you'd expect her to give a start even in the deepest coma. He grins, too, when she flinches, so maliciously, comically threatening her with his finger, as if he had just caught her out alive again. 'Well, Frau Lehmann, how are we today then?' The woman—her sheet, or rather, shroud, reaches up to her chin, her face, sunken, is no more than a shrivelled yellow patch on the white pillow—feebly she says only, 'Och . . .', as if she had nothing further to complain of. It is to be supposed that a male nurse like this must forever be putting on a show of being healthy, not so much to cheer up the patients as far more to fortify himself, to arm himself, so that these ghouls and living dead surging out of doorways all around do not overpower him. In another bed in the corridor lies one who has already had the linen pulled over his face. However, he is not dead. But as he is unable to move his legs or hands he has bitten into the cloth, in order to pull it off his face. It looks like a corpse whose mouth is going on eating, devouring its cover and in the process revealing the feet and then, gradually, bite by bite, the whole naked body . . .

Late in the afternoon—on his second attempt and this time with the approval of the nurse on late-shift—Bekker is finally permitted to see his daughter. He was prepared for a face tired and pale but yet smiling at him. Instead he finds a crooked, abandoned remnant of humanity, so wretched and helpless, hardly conscious, her face surly and tortured, strangely altered and as if thrust back into smallness and childishness. Drips at each wrist, as if her life had to be preserved artificially, from without. . . . Bekker stands there in perplexed, timid pity. Barely has he entered the room (she does not recognize him at all!) but, with a gurgling sound, she demands the basin to throw up in. Her mouth rounds to a babyish pout and her tongue pushes out a frothy white fluid. Then she sinks her glowing head back into the pillow. The drips seem to be heating her unnaturally. 'Open the window,' she commands, softly, groaning. Apparently she was given a strong painkiller for the night, which she cannot take. The morphine has set her a long way back, almost transformed her into another being; the sound of her voice, the whining mood, are exactly those of an ill-behaved little girl. She, whom her father has known recently to be always good-natured, somewhat indifferent, and prepared to put up with things, is now distinctly intolerant, irritable and testy; what little she says always sounds snappy. In her drugged state she seems to feel no more for her dark, declining condition than a small, peevish irritation, as in earlier times when going to the cinema was forbidden her or she had her pocket money docked. She almost makes it difficult to have sympathy with her like that.

Whatever have they done to you, Grit? Yesterday, with the officer's old patent leather case in your hand, wearing a green parka, intact and erect, you still walked through the hospital garden, and now you are wounded, felled, and simply left lying there. It honestly doesn't look as if you're cared for and attended to here. Why does no one look after you? What does Manstett say, what is the word from the chief, what did he find in your back? But nothing can be found out today about the course and result of the operation, and Grit herself cannot know. One thing at least Bekker has happily established—he observed it with some excitement: her legs have already moved, they are not paralysed! However, it is not certain that she herself knows it or whether this her worst fear, that she would come round from the anaesthetic crippled, has not yet in fact recurred to her befogged mind. Suddenly pity surges in him once again, and for a moment he is tempted to tear her recklessly from the drips and bear her away in his arms from this most terrible corner of the underworld. But at this point she again commands, eyes shut: 'Get this blanket off me! . . . For goodness' sake open that window!' It sounds imploring and reproachful. But Bekker hesitates and wonders whether it can be good to expose her weak, overheated body to the air, which by now has grown damper and cooler. Indecisive and cowardly, he murmurs something quite out of place: 'I am only a slave in this institution too. . .'. Now Grit asks to be turned on to her right side, facing the window, for she lacks the strength to do it of her own accord. Again Bekker hesitates, intimidated and apprehensive lest he cause her unbearable pain by some wrong, untrained hold. 'I feel awful,' she groans, 'it hurts so much . . . turn me over . . . open the window.' When her father continues to hesitate and does not dare bring her relief, wanting at all costs to avoid doing something clumsy and inept, she suddenly curses him, quite coarsely and loudly, and with a trembling hand that misses more than once she pushes the bedside bell to summon a nurse to help her. . . . How quickly you have grown crooked, how quickly you have changed, how drastically! Ashamed and lost, Bekker gazes down at Grit's bed, where her head steadily tosses from side to side; and suddenly it seems to him as if this hot, sick body down there in the hollow, in the white, fusty nest, were incubating a wholly strange being, as if this child were becoming transformed into something monstrous. Was it not the Frankensteins that got at her core, poked about in the very nerve-centre of life, if they didn't in fact cut it about and then patch it up any old how? That is by no means a little matter, nothing superficial. Under the knife the fear of death must doubtless always go through the body, in spite of the deep anaesthetized sleep; even if it does not move, nonetheless its

[74]

very being rebels, it screams, it rages, and then perhaps it turns back from those frontiers dimmed and seduced.

That evening Bekker goes about the town again and drinks. He walks—that is, he hops in irregular paces and jumps as he always does when restlessness puts legs on him and his walk speaks a language of pointed exclamations, irascible silence and inflexible hope. . . . You keep going and suddenly you have been passed over. As thousands of millions of particles wander, conjoin and are repulsed. Some sparkle, others don't. Some think, others don't. The play of muscles that gives leeway to thought is not a jot richer than rigor mortis, which has forgotten thought. Both are of no consequence. It is neither here nor there: it all goes on and on. Nothing gets caught up. Bekker sees the nurse gliding in front of him, this bloated boy who wouldn't believe that he was Grit's father and smirked knowingly as he silently drew the catheter out of the pocket of his tunic. This lad will touch her now, she will cling on to his neck and allow him to hoist her on to her other side. Room 18, ward B. The dirty plates on the food trolleys stink in the corridor. . . . Sometimes he runs whispering, and as if he were about to fall from a height, across the straight, level paving, along a dangerous stretch assessed exactly in advance, as if a footbridge or narrow wall-coping were to be crossed, and afterward, relieved, he teeters in a victory pose. Going forward is a feat, it is always a highwire act. He describes a wide semi-circle round approaching passers-by so that their tramping, their waves do not disturb his force-field, his speech, which would promptly lose him his equilibrium. These stumbling ballets and obstacle races become odder and lonelier from bar to bar, the drunker he gets, the more disappointing the company he gets into.

In Claudiusstrasse a man is standing in front of his house flinging accusations at it. A four-storey tenement house dating back to the 1870s but with its façade stripped of all ornamentation, now plastered afresh and cheaply. The man stands rocking on his heels on the kerb and waggling his hands above his head, as if he wanted to shake some calamity out of the air. 'You, house!' he cries in a feeble voice, 'don't drive me to the limit . . . You wretched heap! You've got quite enough to answer for already!' Bekker suddenly stands still as if he'd been tethered to the spot. This shaking of the hands and this 'don't drive me to the limit' comes to him from afar, comes intimately related to smelly gym-shoes, a middle finger knobbly from writing, the bell for break, boys showing their genitals behind high atlases, the fear before and the dread after a test, and all the rest of that jungle that once was school. And 'wretched heap', this stupidest of little phrases, only ever came in this barking way from one mouth, Bongie's mouth. Bongie, biology and chemistry master, and it *is* him too, rocking about at the edge of the street there. My God! does he still live here, number 8 Claudiusstrasse, tormented down to the marrow, settle him, get at him, an awful hooting the moment he entered the class-room, and really he fell for every blessed thing, but why did it have to be him! Na-zi, Na-zi, they all roared in chorus whenever he lost his nerve, hand me the register, don't drive me to the limit, but he really had been a Nazi, everyone knew, and his son Gerhard, who was in our class too and always among the keenest when things got going against his father, gave away the name of his daddy's lover to us, Aschtritt, Aschtritt! the old frump from the Regional Statistics Office, and since Bongie was such an unbelievably good-natured person the persecution naturally extended far into his private life, he simply got back all the wrong the other slave-drivers had done us, he had to do penance for it, the round little flat-footed man, a pink sheet of blotting-paper was fixed to the hem of his jacket at the back with 'I am the nicest Nazi in all——' written on it, and with this he walked leisurely along the streets after school, for outside the establishment he immediately felt fine and adopted a stately and pensive gait which at times he interrupted to reach into the crease of his arse and give himself a pleasurable scratch; at home his wife then began by putting him through it good and proper if he came

[76]

back with something like that blotting-paper at his backside, it is well known that, with Gerhard supplying a bombardment of yells and applause—I was there myself once!—she flung wet laundry and milk-bags at his head, only once did we get him to a point where even our hearts broke, driven once again to the limit he sits down behind his desk, intending to register one name after the other, when suddenly he starts to wail, all of us as one man go 'Ahhhh', genuinely disappointed, genuinely sad, but Gerhard promptly zips behind the desk to his father and puts an arm round his shoulder, but in his hand he holds his little bottle of ink and gingerly dribbles it down Bongie's suit, which the rest of us no longer found so very marvellous, seeing we'd already broken the little Nazi time and time again . . .

So now, Bekker, next to his old teacher on the kerb, is overcome by pangs of penitence and shame, stitches in his side after an exhausting life as after thousand-metre circuits on the school sports ground, he wants to turn to him, beg his forgiveness for so much, and sees that he has become an old man and if appearances are not deceptive is no less plagued by spirits than Bekker himself; Bongie, who takes up a position in front of his house such as he took up in those days before the raging class and tries, with the same helpless despair, the same old phrases, to win respect for himself in the eyes of mute walls which he has inhabited a life long and which he cannot believe to be without a soul that would share their common history.

Bekker calls softly to him: 'Bongie!' The old man looks up at him suspiciously, with timid eyes. Then he shakes his head. No, it is not him, not Bongie any more. Bekker approaches the frightened teacher a pace or so and asks if he cannot remember him, nicknamed the Superbrain, at the Lessing grammar school, in the mid-fifties, in the lower sixth, the newcomer who'd joined the class after he and his mother moved from the Lahn valley. . . . The old man interrupts him and answers joylessly, without considering for a moment:

[77]

'Yes of course.' Then he stares down at the pavement and waits for the danger to pass by. Bekker contemplates him from the side, astonished. All of a sudden the whole tale of undermining humiliation, the execution of this man— stretching out over years—becomes clear to him . . . which he too participated in, the little Superbrain, who would start up 'The International' on sports days, in among the lame ducks, who pricked the Oder-Neisse Line on to aged maps with the point of his compasses and at the same time collaborated with his class teacher, defaming and betraying his fellow-pupils, confident, ambitious for power, prepared for a fight, fretting to and fro impatiently long before the actual start of life, imprisoned far too long in class-rooms, reading rooms and seminars not to run up—with his head crammed with the blind urge to act—against the very next wall, that of Zachler's Institute, and allow himself to be taken into captivity that was to be of the most sublime and lasting kind. Now, fundamentally equal, used and abused, he stands beside this figure of fun from his boyhood, having arrived as it were at the same age as his teacher. With the discreet complicity of two fools, both men, the failed Superbrain and his teacher, raise their eyes in quest of peace up the hemp-coloured façade to the fourth floor, where Bongie always lived.

'A neat little old house,' says Bekker, somewhat stupidly.

'Yes of course,' the teacher quickly concedes, delicately hiding in the protection of agreement. A little later, however, he raises his head and looks into Bekker's face. He frowns slightly, not as if he were endeavouring to recognize his old pupil in the end after all but presumably to find out whether this man next to him is one who thinks fundamentally differently or perhaps not quite differently. Hardly has Bekker met this look than he begins eagerly to talk about old times, although at other times he avoids reminiscence particularly and there is no wallowing in memories. But now all at once Bongie's elaborately-perfected lectures on molecular biology seem unforgettable: at that time in its glittering open stages and not yet textbook wisdom, lessons at the latest scientific level and fascinating, even if it was casting pearls before swine, and only today, at a mature age, can it be assessed—what a silent revolution in the image of man was then proclaimed to a pack of green, screeching louts. . . . In the meantime, though, the old man looks at the ground once more. He does not care to respond to all this and remains silent. After a while, Bekker too having fallen silent again, and keeping his mouth shut, Bongie starts to speak of his own accord, slowly and solely about the house, and with precisely that stiff-necked composure he would adopt in addressing to a staff meeting an application for the removal from the establishment of that incorrigible pupil House. 'Item one. Stairs far too steep. The landing lighting has too short a time-switch phase. Rooms at the front always dark because of church tower in front. Bursts of water-pipes on the agenda. Too many windows looking on to the inner courtyard, too much cleaning. New central heating. Grid gas supply.'

He interrupts himself and scrutinizes Bekker closely, to see whether he is properly able to imagine a renovation of this scope. 'The heating is remote-controlled,' he announces importantly, as if this were the beginning of 1984. As a whole, the house is too much to ask of elderly people such as himself. For this reason, most of the tenants have now moved out. Gloom all round. And the landlord, he says, only installed the heating so that he could raise the rent as staggeringly high as possible, so that in any case it became impossible for the old people to afford to live in this house. And yet, he says, he finds it difficult to forget the house at one go, in spite of all that. So it has become his habit to pass by here in Claudiusstrasse every day, preferably at dusk, sometimes even in the middle of the night.

So the teacher has moved out. For half a year he has been living in the old people's home next to the municipal swimming-pool on the south side. He returns to the subject of the landlord, and after a brief pause, very softly, he says his name: 'Gerhard,' he says, and nods as he says it. Just by saying Gerhard like this the old man quite matter-of-factly gives away that he has known the whole time who Bekker is, for the name Gerhard would mean nothing to a stranger. Oh, Bekker exclaims, what's become of him? What's your son doing? Well, he is a property owner now, he has become a financier, a broker, a powerful man and the owner of a good many houses; this old house is not the only one that belongs to him, which he's thrown his own father out of by shamelessly raising the rent.

Not bad at all. This boy shows quite some staying-power. He persecutes his father with great reserves of strength, unrelentingly to the grave. Truly, there is no slackening of his grip. Gerhard, who had already betrayed and sold his father in front of the class for the sake of a joke, a dirty joke, and at home, impartially, incited his parents against each other, withdrew giggling to safety and watched their brutal kitchen tournaments as voyeurish and transported as if he'd been at the cinema—Gerhard has now delivered one more mighty blow at his father, perhaps the last, to topple the old man at last, the widower and pensioner, this man who has already been robbed and wounded in so many ways. Tremendous wickedness—not bad at all. A son has here devised for his progenitor a patient enterprise in destruction, planned far-sightedly, for which he had first to acquire a position and power, first to become his father's landlord, to carry it out fully. To get at Zachler like that! To strangle him so long like that. . . . But you can only torment someone for a long time that you have power over. If you are powerless and thrown on your own resources, all that is left you is a brief attack, the sniper's shot, assassination—all manner of rapid actions in which evil can never attain to its full unfolding, for this can only be achieved in open-ended continuity, the inescapable torment constantly resuming.

Bekker is anxious to hear his old teacher speak once again, lead him back on to the overgrown paths of the class-room. And he would like to assure him that that last lesson on a Saturday noon, when he tried to introduce the secrets of life amid stinking, howling and a hail of paper darts, was not

[80]

utterly in vain. This much-tried scholar, then freshly cleansed of the bloodthirsty twaddle of Nazi racism, took to flight in a forward direction, so to speak, by caring only to proclaim the latest, exactest and most progressive in his field—he ought to know that he was not preaching to deaf ears.

'What are the latest developments in the field of molecular biology?' asks Bekker eagerly. 'What do the creators of our world-image say today? Have you found out enough new things?'

'Yes of course,' the old man says again, and promptly slips back into silence.

'Listen, Bongie: if we follow up in our mind the things we know today about the origins of life—in philosophy, I mean—mankind is gradually robbed of all its consolations and sinks from century to century in its own self-esteem. Weren't you amply amused, already in those days, by the false, historical materialists, the humanists, who consider mankind so over-important? I remember well what you thought of them—nothing at all, absolutely nothing. And once you even said: these thinkers of mankind and the human condition today represent something similar to what Hegel was at one time for Marx—only a hothead, the whole of dialectical materialism, while the genetic code supplies the secure feet for it—even if they are those of a quite different living being! You permitted yourself a joke like that back in those days, and you yourself laughed heartily at it, your shoulders shaking, quite by yourself, since no one was listening after all. Now we must know of the pre-biotic soup out of which life originated on earth, a contact of carbons, water and ammoniac that was dictated wholly by chance and perhaps was even unique, a combination which, as far as we can tell in the corner of the universe we have access to, these ten thousand million galaxies we can view through our telescopes and tune in to from earth, does not exist a second time. Now we must know that a simple bacteria cell is equipped with the same chemical structure and uses the same genetic code as is responsible for the structure of the human organism. We must know that the evolution of species did not proceed in fulfilment of a pre-ordained plan at

[81]

whose terminal point stood this being Man, but rather that every development in the biosphere had its origin in the typing errors of genetic transmission, in pure chance, blunders, breakdowns in the duplication process—for the ambition, the dream of every living cell is to duplicate itself identically and nothing else. All changes are fundamentally mistakes occasioned by mutation and tested by selection. A world-view of this nature is nothing for kids, nor for Christians, and assuredly not for Marxists. It jeopardizes all philosophies that place Man at their centres, by proclaiming the true incidental quality of his existence in natural history. And if Man—in Monod's famous words—if Man were to accept the truth, this truth of his biosphere, he would need to awake at last from that thousand-year sleep of ideologies and religions and recognize his total abandonment, his totally peripheral role. He needs to know that he occupies his place like a gypsy at the edge of the universe, and the universe is deaf to his music and indifferent to his hopes, suffering or crimes. . . .'

As a pause now follows, in which Bekker reflects on his own words, affected by a world-picture of this kind as much as by the endless starry sky, the old man all at once slowly shakes his head, to make a reservation, laboriously and not yet quite decided about it.

'Knowledge,' he says, 'knowledge can of course always be known. That is not the point. You can maintain something, young man, you know a good deal. But I—I have to keep the house and the whole opposite of knowledge before my eyes all the time.' After these words he bows slightly and turns to go. Bekker holds him back, and the old man remains standing like a pupil caught by the nape of the neck.

'Wait, Bongie. . . . But if the basis of Everything were mud, blackness, and not a picture at all, and only Man holds his little light by which everything appears light and is yet a will-o'-the-wisp . . . then thinkers today must really ask: where does this leave you? the beloved subject of world history, the holy I? And: hasn't this last century just made a beginning at discovering the laws of language, of the mind, the language of genetics and of the unconscious, at describing them as systems of rules which operate independently of the thinking subject and his changing locations and which are as universal and capricious as natural laws? There is information and language in everything, from the tiniest bacteria cell to the most secret tip of a dream, we are filled beyond capacity with micro-texts, codes and alphabets, languages everywhere and all manner of rule by law and alien forms of order. How could there still be room left over for an I? Thus it is that even for the philosopher the human subject has changed from the most sublime to the most boring object of his contemplation. Man? he says, forget it. The human being, that perpetual number one of world history? Forget it. This being is finally starting to figure out the operation of the rules to which he owes his appearance in history. By now he at least knows this much: that this same operation of the rules will also take him out of history again. The wind will blow a long time after we have ceased to be. And the codes will go their unfathomable way. But we will silt up with sand, drifted over like a heap of shit on the beach. But before that, Bongie, the things will first overtake us, the inanimate will rob us of power. For one morning, Bongie, it will be the things that have dragged the speech from our throats. One morning in the garden a spat-out piece of chewing-gum will awaken under the barbecue grill and stretch. Suddenly, lo, he hears above him, veritably, he hears the grill—talking! And practically at the same moment, a primaeval taking of breath, a thrust of Creation and the chewing-gum speaks too: "Is that you talking?" he asks the grill.

"Yes," says the grill, "I'm talking. I'm talking perfectly."

"Me too," says the chewing-gum, and is astonished.

"What's it like, talking?" asks the grill from up top.

"Fine, thanks," replies the chewing-gum lightly, "so now we have language."

The grill: "Now we have our entertainment for ever."

The chewing-gum: "And how is Man? What is his opinion about it?"

[83]

The grill: "Man? Man's standing there with his mouth open. Come to a standstill. Dried up. Exhausted with his mouth open."

The chewing-gum: "It had to happen sooner or later. The hard fall back into matter. Loses his stories, his words, his mind."

The grill: "The human being. What's left of number one? A natural sound, produced by the wind howling in his open mouth . . ."

'There you have it, Bongie, things talking among themselves. But we stand stiff and mute and think the way snow falls. After all, we have accumulated far too many forms of order, we've piled them up wildly on top of each other and have put a startling excess of meaning into the world. Too much logic, too many proofs, experiences, too much reason, for the whole thing not to end in the most tangled and primitive kind of chaos. Chaos, the as yet still suppressed speech of the whole, mere tumult, but everywhere pushing more powerfully to the fore. When once that grows loud, when one day it is no longer possible to rule and regulate and anarchy is reality, the individual will at first reel under an immense pressure and his sense of history will burst like an eardrum, so that he will suddenly stand before his telephone, at a loss, swinging the receiver, pushing it about as a dog pushes a plastic bone, not even remotely knowing what it is or what you do with it, with this bent bit. In this way the meanings of the most domestic of apparatus again become defamiliarized, and it may be that the chartered accountant with dazzling skills in six programming languages will strip down overnight, layer by layer, to the God-fearing copperplate engraver that this vain contemporary had once been in an earlier existence, to be exact at the court of Duke Anton Ulrich in Brunswick. That past craft, that bygone patience again takes him over and he becomes incapable of looking at the road without an abysmal dizziness or of bearing the speeds on the road. It is not as if it were only the ghostly flitting of the vehicles—even the very walk, the simple, unmeasured, obsessed walk of the pedestrians, would be enough to drive him stark mad. The most ordinary sound in the heating pipes swells into the booming drone of the beyond. The German of the contemporary world: only distantly and half comprehensible, in a tormenting way. Thus the whole body falls apart along with its conditions, the soul and things fall rumblingly apart. The suddenly aged man loses his footing all round. In the end he tries to hide under blankets and pillows, without finding protection there, for the stench of the chemical fibres constantly provokes nausea. He cannot go anywhere any more. He is more afraid than one person alone. His horror is that of a unique freak and five-headed monster of his species, got rid of and abandoned on another planet. . . .'

I don't normally like walking about in one of the remoter parts of town. Nothing really tempts me to go there. Most outskirts have little life of their own. Young people go into the town centre, the old sleep or stare at television. In the pubs on the corner the men all know each other and I get no pleasure out of pushing my way in among them. But today after my hospital visit, and all the more after that strange reunion in Claudiusstrasse, I had to go down to the canal, and I followed its ramrod course leading out of town. Almost flight from the busy streets and squares, among other things because—on top of everything else—certain kinds of nuisance have been becoming noticeably more frequent there of late. I don't know what causes it but more and more people, elderly people, are pursuing a peculiar pastime or an irresistible desire and have an absolute need to say something to a complete stranger or find some fault with him. They busy themselves about you with all manner of needless, unembarrassed comments. 'Why are you wearing that traditional jacket, in this weather?' a woman from a fast-food stall, her wig askew, calls across to me. Others say: 'You still have some toothpaste in the corner of your mouth, right there', or 'You look like Adenauer'. It is terrible, the disease is spreading, and no one knows where it

[85]

originates. Passers-by fly at your face like moths at a lit-up window. They're not actually interested in anything, they just want to pluck some fluff off someone. Some of them, I guess, begin to be affected by an increased urge to communicate the moment their feet touch the pavement and the general pell-mell out on the street befuddles them. Others stop, standing in front of you, merely to have a good groan. You'd think the way the earth beneath its thickly-coated asphalt struggles for air had got into their bodies. Down here on the bank of the canal it is by contrast more peaceful. The frayed-out end of an industrial estate, hardly any traffic at this time. Yet how little that helps when restlessness is shaking your bones from within. In this of all states of mind, feeling fundamentally unforgiving, I must needs stumble upon a cripple—that irregular tap-tap, you hear it even at a distance!—who drags himself along the promenade in the dark, infinitely heavily and slowly, by means of a kind of play-pen constructed of several walking-sticks. He appears, a hideous remnant of humanity, an accident freak, amputated to under his brow, and hauls his abnormally leisurely world towards me, disturbs my walk, tormenting me quite simply by his contrary tempo. Yes, I am in a hurry, I am troubled, burdened with worries, and this handicapped fellow is handicapping *me*, inconsiderately, and that uneven walk of his, utterly his own, unchangeable, seems rebellious to me. What do you do in a department store when you know where you want to head for, quickly, and someone walking at a leisurely pace blocks your way? You cuff your way angrily past him, you're looking for and need the provocation. Inappropriate tempos can provoke you worse than stupid words. In any case, if you walk such a lot you are surrounded by the most varied speeds on all sides. Each and every thing has its very own measure of time, a waving branch has a different one from the flowing canal, the bus thundering by a different one from the dripping mouth of a fountain, not to mention the ultimate haste of light, of sound, of . . . you are, so to speak, caught in a chaotic volley of missiles of time, and only a being very intent on its goal and highly resistant

[86]

will always come through unharmed and, in spite of all walking, still be able to rest peacefully in itself.

The cripple, of whom little remains, practically no face, only flat white skin transplanted up there from his thighs or back, hairless, with neither lips nor ears nor nose, but with artificial teeth screwed into his shattered jaw and sticking out of his open hole of a mouth, and with orthopaedic claws where his hands used to be, with high, tightly-laced boots on his artificial legs—this man, who no doubt only comes out at night, his black, broad-brimmed hat pulled over his forehead, and, since there must needs be this stylish hat, for protection, there is also beneath it a fine silk scarf and, matching it, likewise inconspicuously elegant, his long, waist-fitting cashmere coat, so that he truly appears to relish looking a gentleman in his play-pen, down to the last collar-stud—this man has, by the by, clearly been able to get used to every limitation, all but one: that the very sight of him sends a shudder through every living soul. He will never come to terms with that: forever to see only faces full of horror and loathing whenever he wants to look at someone and raises his lashless eyelids. Yet that he, as one with all the time in the world, arouses rebellious feelings in other people who are in a hurry—this I now observe in a walker who appears behind him too, one who is on his way with quite especial haste, in a sloppy, casual-wear jacket and slippers, straight from his living-room, a walkie-talkie with a waggly aerial pressed to his cheek: he has raced out in the midst of the international match on account of a trip to the mailbox he can't put off. His wife has to keep him informed while he is away by means of this walkie-talkie, supplying him with a report, not merely by passing on what the meagre TV commentary has to offer but by adding something more; indeed, like a radio commentator she also has to represent the rising action with an excited voice so that her husband can remain connected to the tension on the pitch while he is away. I can see how irritable he becomes at that very point where he overtakes the dragging fellow, how he angrily jumps to one side, angry perhaps because his wife in front of the screen is offering an uncertain report about whether it is a free kick or a penalty for the Spanish and he therefore has to ask about it fiercely, but angry without a doubt because in overtaking it is as if he were hit by an electric shock, where the friction of the unsynchronized tempos of these two walkers is discharged, and he does not so much jump aside, voluntarily and embittered, as get thrown.

Turning away from the canal some time later and across to the office area of town, which until recently was completely empty of people at night, stone-dead and with a host of traffic lights and neon lights lit up for no one, and into whose fantastic grave-like silence I had at times dared to venture. In the meantime the city fathers have filled some empty high-rises, written-off ruins, with flats, have seen to it that there is a row of shops, restaurants and a cinema and other facilities which only appear to revivify. I have to pause in front of a Design Centre. Immediately opposite, across the road, there is another centre, a Laundry Centre. So nowadays everything is called centre this and centre that, increasingly so in proportion to the town's lack of a middle. The designers have begun to design right in front of their store. The parking lines have been interrupted there and a little area with bright white pebbles filled in. From this area there arise, as in a botanical garden in the 5th galaxy, a number of street lamps of visionary form, glowing all over the place. Next to the futuristic ones there is an old three-armed candelabrum for comparison too, so that you see how everything has ceaselessly developed. One of the futuristic ones towers especially high, resembling the mighty crosier of a bishop. The shaft is of dark, broad-edged steel, and a large glass globe balances like a luminous pearl on the sea of the spiral bend. The other models are less majestic, seem partly to be more powerfully inspired by sombre animal fantasies than by a sober understanding of form, like, for example, that two-armed beast with its many elongated compound eyes, which sprays light around as if through a very fine atomizer. I cannot pass by these lamps of tomorrow without wondering sadly from which of them friend Ortlepp would have strung himself up, if restlessness had driven him—as it did that time, that icy-cold January night—into this office part of town and before this grotesque selection. . . . The completed puzzle-books were sticking out of both his jacket pockets as he hung there on high, head bowed. An Ortlepp would know whither. He always did know. The only enemy of Zachler, the only spirit in the Institute that didn't ape the boss. There is a restlessness that only a noose can put an end to. I find it more comprehensible than ever, that he needed to get up there on the bars, high up next to the lamps, and didn't allow water to beguile him at all, didn't care to slink in there as the defeated and melancholy try to do, nor wished to fall either, to fly right down to the depths. . . . 'He doesn't know what to do with his energy', how often I still hear Zachler's disparaging estimate of the uncomfortable Ortlepp. But, my boss, he did know, as you can well see!

I order my cognac in a newly-appointed pizzeria, right next to the designers' place, but all they serve is a miserable German brandy. From my table I have a view of the brightly-lit coin-op laundry and the many rolling and spinning drums of the washing-machines. Late in the evening a good deal is still being washed there. Mostly they are men that are sitting there, reading books and waiting for their laundry. Nonetheless, it looks anything but a social meeting-place over there. None of them speaks to the others. Yes indeed, how everything has ceaselessly gone on developing. Wasn't washing, washing in particular, a scene of cheerful gossip and song—once upon a time, so they say—when women were alone together at ponds or wells?

At the next table two married couples are sitting across from each other, all the same age, about fifty. The two women are of ample girth and both wear large, very large spectacles. One couple is German, the other is from Denmark. Holiday acquaintances, hearty neighbours in caravans, ending with an exchange of addresses, gushing invitations, definitely a reunion; and now it has come alarmingly true, the Danes are there, though only passing through *en route* for the south. They use the familiar form of address but their looks remain uncertain, above all those of the Danes, who after that last summer at Bornholm are at a loss to know what to make of the joyless matter-of-factness that the Germans now reveal on home ground, in their own town and not on holiday. The Germans talk exclusively about themselves, and build up their numerous opinions around them like a fortress. The husband praises the family. It is the best thing you can have in the world. Everything else is increasingly becoming of no consequence to him, a dismissive hand gesture. The Dane listens with effort and says, his eyes unmovingly fixed on that distant acquaintance: 'Yes . . . yes . . . yes', rather too frequently, softly, and preferring one yes too many to risking, by some question, snapping the other's thread of speech and patience, for how quickly anyone will become angry if required to repeat himself. The Danes have to drink Lambrusco. Lambrusco tastes like cherry wine, say the Germans, intending to initiate the northerners into this Italian taste. In fact, everything they say, the more slowly and clearly they pronounce it, sounds the more superior and didactic. At the very moment the Germans' will to communicate is at its most unrelenting, they patronizingly rob the foreigners of speech, without intending it; and by needing to use their own language more and more makeshiftly, unsubtly, with mistakes, they find their guests more and more of a burden, so that soon they speak to them as they would to ignorant children or the mentally retarded and in the end in fact consider them to be such. So it is not surprising that the Danes become constantly more shy and insecure. On top of this, the Germans find it difficult to listen, since this demands a certain sub-missiveness of manner, and they are prepared to play this role only very negligently, if not in fact unwillingly. Nevertheless, the Danish woman, who is least competent in German, insists on telling a story. Meanwhile, however, the food has arrived, minestrone, providing a distraction from each other, which the Germans welcome. But this makes concentration more difficult for the Danish woman. She only looks once, briefly, at the dish placed before her, shoves her spoon absently under the napkin and persists in her halting speech. With every word, hardly is it out but she doubts it again. 'The train . . . came—came?' 'Yes, the train came', the German assures her, curtly, coarsely, not looking at her, and takes the little dish of Parmesan from his wife's hand. 'The train came southish . . . um, southly from . . .' After the shortest of periods the German woman, to whom this is being directly addressed, loses all control and without further ado stops listening. She spoons into the minestrone, with no eyes any more for the Danish woman, whom she ruthlessly leaves in mid-sentence, to wallow in a flowing speech of her own, enthusing about minestrone, about the Pizzeria Giovanni, the vegetable soup that she sometimes prepares at home too, and as she speaks she aims her every word sideways at her husband, where home and the same language are. The Danish woman's raised arm with its hand open for emphasis remains up in the air for a long time, strangely long and forgotten, the sad ruin of a perished story, and now she too—without, however, actually expecting help—looks at her husband, who is supping minestrone and pays her no attention. For his part, he has seemed for some time to be preparing something that he intends to say in German presently. Briefly, the two exchange a few words in Danish. This sounds suddenly so transformed and healthy, so artistically vigorous, that the Germans look up with curiosity from their plates. Then the Dane turns to the German and says: 'The soup is good.' As the joint opinion of himself and his wife. Cautiously and quietly he adds: 'The wine is very sweet,' clearly no friend of Lambrusco. The German instantly raises his glass and calls it a glass of fiery wine. 'Yes, it is sweet. Sweet and dry. A typical Italian homegrown wine.' He had ordered a whole litre of it without first consulting the Dane. At that moment, as I beckon for a second brandy, a girl comes

[91]

from where she has been sitting a while alone at the back and takes up a position straight in front of my table.

She is wearing a wide cape-like raincoat buttoned up to the collar-bone. Without greeting me she asks if I am prepared to accompany her home through the nearby park, just as soon as she has collected her washing from across the road. She stands sulkily, almost reproachfully in front of me, with her eyes cast down, abashed by too much courage, just as if I had spoken to her and not the other way round.

'You can see I'm sitting here drinking my cognac.'

'Sure. But still. Will you?'

She says she is afraid of the foreigners, 'the Arabs', as if this meant both the worst of strangers and, in a higher sense, strangers in general. She asks if she can sit at my table for the time being.

I hate unwanted company. I hate small talk: the smaller it is, the more effort it demands. Desperately you try to remain unacquainted with each other: what do I ask now? What else might interest me? What else is there which is of no importance and which we haven't yet mentioned? . . . And she does seem rather odd to me, and oddness, when it is emphasized in this way, holds little attraction for me.

As she stands there before me, and I do not answer, I think: what a simple soul, and she wants to play the self-confident, opportunist, liberated woman! But you notice it, such a little awareness, quite confused by the all too difficult struggle for self-awareness, which has yet always remained bottomless and will so remain. And just now she tried to make a start, sailed clean across her own shadow, and really she has already slipped over. To approach a strange man so aggressively and demand that he give you his company by way of protection: there is a contradiction in this. 'At other times you can't see straight with anyone, you. . . !' I should like best of all to shout this at her. Yes, I am tempted to wound her, her of all people, a patent innocent and beginner, wound her in her sex-war honour, so that at least one of them will for once get to feel that their horde cannot forever trample on our kind with impunity, and some time sooner or later they can expect no more help from us, when they just happen to need someone . . . let them see how they manage on their own, these solidarity–cunts . . . Oh, I find it all so very welcome, if only it really is a fight, instead of suffocating in this messed–up, dirty, lying world of *relationships*! . . . She simply stands there. She stands at my table and waits for me to say yes at last and offer her a seat. The waiter comes and does not know where to serve the espresso she has ordered. Fine. Now the waiter is waiting at my table too. I can stick it out. I look past them both and across at the washing–machines, where there is such a lively racing and rolling, stopping and going. Arabs! Let her take a taxi. I'm not afraid to walk through even the worst corner of town. I have never really been afraid of being attacked by a foreigner, and in countries where they do not speak German, in the foreign quarters of our own cities too, I in fact feel completely safe from physical threat. Only those that speak German can do anything to me. All my suspicion, and even a secret fear of death, is focused on those alone who are intimates or friends. 'Do sit down.'

So the espresso is served at my table. Her dark blonde hair is very thin and with her fingertips she combs it behind her ear again and again on the side turned towards me. Now that she is sitting next to me, after her test of courage, her trembling and embarrassment set in. Her ear is relentlessly exposed, and as it is a lovely ear, delicately formed, the gesture may well mean both: a little exposure, temptation, as well as fearful attentiveness, so as to understand quite correctly now, at all costs, unimpeded by the curtain of hair, just don't mishear anything.

I think of Grit in hospital, and with a worry like that, what this idiosyncratic woman at my table actually signifies is really a matter of indifference to me. She squeezes the little carton of milk violently and shakily into her espresso, so that it makes a repellent, obscene, juicy smacking sound. A jet of it sprays right across her coat. 'These things,' she exclaims, outraged, making believe her blush of shame is a blush of anger, 'you usually just get these things in trains!' She cleans her spattered coat with a paper handkerchief. Then she asks what I actually think of her 'audacity', was I scandalized or something.

'No. You can sit down wherever you want.'

'You looked so sad. Are you sad?'

'No. I'm tired.'

She asks if I have so much work to do during the day, to make me so tired at night. No reply. She is a secretary in a lawyer's office. Yesterday her boss went on a trip for a day or so, so she can divide her workload up as she wants and needn't be tired in the evening. Everything she utters is sufficiently familiar and merits no particular interest. And yet I order myself: look at her, listen, don't be miserly with your sympathy because you are not entitled to be. We are One Suffering, One Wish, One Failure. So a little smart-alickness and the many bubbling blisters in your mouth make little difference. We are all dabbling about in the same pool.

'My boss has big, dark brown eyes.'

Then she asks about my job and immediately adds, as if to pacify me, that she has to go in a minute or two, the washing has just been spun dry. I answer her briefly as possible.

'Officer. Soldier. I *was* an officer, a soldier.'

'In the army?'

'Where else.'

Her 'partnership' with a young doctor broke up last week, she says. He wasn't able, or willing, to speak to her. For example, after they'd been to the theatre, to see Sternheim's *The Trousers*, she'd liked it but he'd been left completely silent. 'Perhaps we were two different worlds.'

Now she wants to know after all why I am no longer in the army.

'Leave me alone!'

She flinches and cowers over her coffee. She says nothing. The familiarity and the loud rebuke have shocked her and made her somewhat easier, more sociable. She pulls her purse and key-ring out of her coat pocket and places both on the table, so that I see it won't be much longer till I'm rid of her. From the key-ring there hangs a small alarm-whistle, no doubt to frighten off thieves and protect her from rape. She drinks up her espresso, holding the back of her hand under the cup although it is not dripping, and at last, her head still bowed over her cup, she dares another question, timorously but irrepressibly: whether I am living in a partnership. . . .

No.

Do I know what to do with myself, in the evenings in particular? Yes, I say, yes. And all at once it sounds peaceful and shaded over, as if I'd been giving this woman the answers to many questions for many years already. After a while I even say, completely hollow and absent: 'Oh well. Who knows what'll turn up.' These first words that have not been extorted from me but have trickled out on their own give her the courage for further blether. For a while she had a problem struggling against secret drinking, above all in the evenings. In fact I have been noticing this for some time from her body, her peculiar restlessness, the trembling controlled with effort, her upper half cowering forward and back in that way women that drink have when they are ashamed of their addiction. Then she puts two one-mark coins by the espresso cup and stands up. She looks straight into my face. She asks somewhat bitterly, and reviewing everything once again: 'Has this ever happened to you before?' And I reply: 'Yes,' although it is not the case, but it simply sounds so mild and indifferent, and No would certainly have sounded far too abrupt.

'Well, then it can't have been so bad.'

She goes. But after a few paces she turns round again. She stands in my line of vision and unbuttons her coat from the bottom to the top and spreads it open wide. She shows me her high, round belly with the white shirt-tails sticking out away from it. She is pregnant. Now she smiles, so proudly and brilliantly, triumphing over all her losses, humiliations and bungling, that I should like to disappear for shame and dizziness. What a mistake, what a mean failure to see the real situation! Every conclusion I came to about this creature was wrong. She is pregnant, she is with child, she has hope. It was only my own malice, my distrust, my revulsion that

[95]

diminished her to an irksome, twaddling typist, and now, after she has arisen from the cast-off remains of the poor miss in the form of the blessed bride, I feel only the urge to submit contritely to her, the pregnant one, to her natural superiority, her beauty, her pride. How confident she is, standing there, showing me her happiness! Not to punish me or painfully dazzle me, but so that I might still take pleasure in her and discover that a sprayed milk carton, an embarrassed conversation, a stupid enthusiasm for her boss, all that is inadequate in her, is completely annihilated in this image of strength and assurance, of the approaching end of loneliness. Now she turns away before I can open my mouth again. I hesitate to run after her. No, I have no right to hold her up, here I've blown everything, shown no instinct, I have behaved blindly, contrary to nature. She crosses the street to the launderette. Her hands in her coat pockets, she strides away in unassailable peace, erect, her head held high. And yet—and yet she is afraid to walk through the park alone tonight, she is afraid of Arabs! How could I refuse her my help! Now she will ask someone else to accompany her. Immovably stiff in my conversion, deprived of my peace, I sit at the table looking after her.

At the north side of the hospital couples step out in a loose *ronde* on to the balconies, visitors and patients who have long been separated, frequently the same picture of embracing, on every storey, they press close to each other, openly and hardly embarrassed, exposing themselves, so lightly-clad, to the cool air simply in order to escape those rooms where several patients lie, where everything is observed and listened to by fellow-sufferers with whom one has, true, struck up a friendship in many respects, who nonetheless revert to squinting strangers as soon as visitors arrive. The couples lean against the balcony parapets. One woman in a dressing-gown, wearing only a night-dress under it, pushes her visitor ahead of her—seriously, directly, under compulsion—in such a way that they can touch, at least a little, and once again have to practise the squeezing and caressing, the movements of love, of the earliest, barred-up times.

Today, on the second day, Bekker finds his daughter in a somewhat improved condition. At least she is awake and fully conscious. Her face, however, is reddened from a good deal of crying. The surgeon-in-chief and the assistant medical director came to see her a while before and informed her of the result of the operation. Grit, her mouth and chin twisting as she softly sobs, says: 'It was all for nothing.' What? What was for nothing? 'Everything. Why did you drag me to this bloody clinic? What are you doing to me?' It sounds so despairing and accusing—as if she were genuinely convinced that her father is in league with the doctors and is sacrificing her for an evil, malicious experiment. Bekker is deeply shocked by the reproachful tone, and immediately is seized once more by the guilty feeling that he was never a proper father to her but always the helpless, devious observer spying on his child, and thus indeed harmful to her. He also doubts whether the feeling of responsibility for Grit which has so uplifted him recently is actually genuine, and not rather a complacent one, artificially induced. How, after so many years of inner desolation, hatred, rawness and inconsiderateness, should he still be capable of love and care? He had somehow lost the knack of looking naturally at this person, of seeing his own child in her. He senses a sharp lack, an absence of real fatherhood, in every moment, every mannerism, relaxed, strict and affectionate, deeply involved and sensible—not being a father in a taken-for-granted and total way, in such a way as if The Father existed as an absolute figure, completely secure in nature.

Grit claims the doctors did as good as nothing. They punctured two radicular cysts, the biggest ones, and cerebro-spinal fluid flowed out of them, and they removed two little bones, so that all the other cysts—how many dozen still clustered down there by the vertebra!—so that these things should have more room and not put such strong pressure on the nerves. . . . Bekker cannot believe that Grit listened to the doctors properly or understood their explanations adequately. He asks the matron to arrange a talk with Manstett, the chief, for him. (Grit too already frequently calls him the chief, as if she were employed here.) But Manstett has already left the building. Instead, the assistant director receives him in his room. He takes time out for Bekker, even has coffee brought for them and offers cigarettes. Yes, it is true, unfortunately they were only able to perform a superficial operation on this patient, alas. Basically, nothing more extensive could be done. The assistant director explains to Bekker, using X-ray photos, what kind of condition he must imagine they found in that lowest segment of Grit's spinal cord. Evidently he is proud of the idiosyncratic manner of speaking he has adopted for conversations with laymen, an unbearable mixture of humorous, flippant turns of phrase and clinically frosty technical jargon, which he then promptly translates. 'The cauda equina, the pony-tail of the spinal cord, beset with a veritable horde of cysts, these doughy bags there, looks just like a tree full of ravioli. . . . It would be an endless finicky affair but under certain circumstances, in theory, the cysts could have been completely or nearly completely removed. But in this hospital we do not do such things on principle. The chief—' 'Why not?' asks Bekker brusquely. There is a suspicion that Grit's incomplete treatment might even in the end prove to be due to the laziness of the doctors or to a special school of neuro–surgery standing on limited principle. 'It's like this: the chief is of the opinion that the risk of paraparesis, paralysis of both legs, is too great with such an operation. We know too little about the origins of these cysts, we don't know how long it has taken them to turn into what they are today. Some of the attendant symptoms go back to early puberty. The claw foot and probably the beginning of a slackening of the muscles in the lower left leg. Not till later did the increased disturbance of the sphincter muscle set in, the muscle that closes the bladder and rectum. Ditto the pigmentation disorder on the behind and, lastly, the chronic inflammation of the renal pelvis. We don't know how or why these cysts originally came to be formed. We can now definitely rule out a malignant growth, since this mass of cysts has accumulated over an extraordinarily long period of time and it is perfectly possible that this process will come to a stop of its own accord, or has already done so. As to the laminectomy—there we took out two vertebral arches that the human skeleton can quite happily do without—all we're aiming at is to give a bit of elbow-room to all those little creatures down there. Let's hope that the pressure on the nerve tissue is gradually eased off now and the symptoms slacken off. For the moment, our motto must be: wait and see, and keep an eye on things. We cannot expect perceptible reactions before six to nine months have passed. Nerves are slow on the uptake, so to speak. It takes time till they notice the pressure is off them again.'

The assistant director leans back and lays the X-ray photos aside. Then he assesses Bekker through eyes suddenly narrowed behind his tinted glasses. It looks as if he feels the urge to confront this unknown visitor abruptly with something totally different, something very personal or else something completely ordinary, at any rate something that has nothing to do with the matter in hand. It is the same kind of pinched look you are familiar with from men who size you up at the bar to see whether you'd be suitable for their dirty jokes, who are irresistibly tempted to lay their stinking spoor, and aim to entice you by this means into an alliance.

'I don't know what your opinion is,' says the assistant director, 'but isn't it astounding? There you have them, on the one hand these red hordes, these poisoners—here in this place of ours as well, you won't have failed to notice it, if you took a look at the scrawl in the lift, those shit-house slogans about a classless hospital and so on and so forth. And on the other hand a quite colossal need is growing, among young people in particular, for political leadership that they are able to see as positive, at long last, quite simply positive. I mean, it's self-evident that they'll grow more and more apathetic towards our state, it doesn't grip them, emotionally there's nothing in it. I know a lot of young people who feel a genuine lack of a

[99]

political home. And a lot of them are simply fed up with just switching on a critical distance the moment they hear the word "state". They want to feel something like warmth for once, belonging, identification, enthusiasm too. There were some only recently here in the house who were enthusiastic over Khomeini, tears in their eyes, Germans, not Persians, young men, raving about this gloomy old crock down there in far-off Iran. And why? Because it's okay to love him, you see, because the masses really love him. This craving for some kind of political love, this craving for belonging, can't be throttled off in the long run, it can't be neutralized, it can't even be replaced by private commitments, love for your family, a house or garden or football pitch. Something much deeper is needed. Don't get me wrong—this isn't any party line I'm pushing. For fifteen years, ever since my storm-and-stress phase in the SHB* I've looked neither right nor left. I merely observe, I listen, as a critical contemporary, as a doctor who doesn't just cure people when they're poorly but gets to hear a whole lot and is in on upheavals of the spirit that maybe don't become so clearly apparent out there in normal, (in inverted commas!) healthy life.'

Bekker steals a very cold, sidelong glance at the assistant director, who is about his own age and will never make it to surgeon-in-chief. He doubts whether he need answer a man who, as soon as he has taken one step beyond the limits of his own field, lapses into blubbering gibberish and drags down with him all the authority he had a moment ago, as a doctor. How can this proceed from one and the same brain? Is this stupidity not also ultimately involved in the doctor's knowledge, in formulating judgements, diagnoses, in acting? Deadly dangerous. And yet as things turn out he cannot resist laying his own stinking spoor as well. Without feeling any inner agitation he counters: 'The state is an ice-cold self-abuse machine. No one who is capable of love will love anything like it. If they did, specialists in suffocation in national con-flagrations would start arriving by land, sea and air. Plonk!—

* Sozialistischer Hochschulbund, a left-wing student organization.

like Icarus. From every storey the intellectuals would fall like cans into the rubbish skips. At least return the empties, you guzzlers of mankind!'

The assistant director slides about on his chair and breathes in through his clenched teeth with a hiss. Bekker leans forward and adds rather more emphatically: 'Destroy, I mean, destroy.'

The assistant director says hastily, fending Bekker off with his hand: 'Fine. That's fine, Mr—' Then he swivels in his chair towards the window and looks out for a while. 'Ha!'—he exclaims suddenly, from the depths of a suppressed passion. And again: 'Ha!'— his gaze still directed out of the window. Then he swivels back in his chair and once more turns directly to Bekker. 'The way I see it, you're in the right place here with views like that. Destroy, destroy. You're really something, Mr—.Just suppose that in the operating-theatre yesterday morning we'd approached your daughter with views like yours, there you go, it's not as simple as that, my dear chap. Okay. I can only ask you to urge your daughter once again not to grow reckless and impatient. When all's said and done we must be quite clear about it: she is in a relatively advanced stage of nerve damage which, if we are to avert worse to come, requires regular check-ups and above all the immediate commencement of urological treatment. I had the impression she was disappointed by the (in inverted commas!) lack of success of the operation, and would rather leave here today than tomorrow and forget the whole affair. I on the contrary consider it imperative that she should remain for observation for at least two to three weeks and afterwards be thoroughly examined by Urology so that something can be done as fast as possible about the residual urine. But you know, of course, the patient can do or not do whatever she considers right. We can't force anyone. Therapy always takes two . . .'

Grit's tears flow silently and evenly, falling together with snot always on the same sodden spot on the pillow. She has lain on her right since the early morning, with a view from the ninth floor of a low, grey, snow-laden sky which, however, releases nothing, and which reflects a dirty yellow glow from the lights of the town. Of the town itself she can see nothing from her position. She wants to ring for the nurse, and she suddenly thinks, for the first time, that she might be able to do something in the pot, alone, without a catheter. She requests her father to go out and wait. But this time Bekker insists on helping her himself. She places both arms around his shoulders so that he can raise her a little, pull up her night-dress and shove the bedpan under her. Then she tries to let go, reaches for the bar hanging above her, pulls her upper half up, gasping with pain, and wedges herself fast with her shoulders. She herself is staggered by the extent of her disability, and her eyes, reddened from crying, open wide. Bekker turns his head to the window so that for a few seconds he need not watch his child, this little figure alive with so many eloquent movements, having to contort herself with effort now, like a cripple. 'Hold me!' Grit's arm slips across the bar, she is not strong enough to cling on. Her father takes hold of her from in front and puts her arms around his neck. They embrace each other exactly like lovers. And yet, this is a clasp of help and need, and the meaningful waiting is all for a little pee and quite distracts them from each other. Bekker stands awkwardly bowed and tensed, his crossed legs press against the edge of the bed and the backs of his knees begin to tremble. 'Not so hard . . . careful!' Her whole body is one single rigid will to break through the barrier, to squeeze water from her abdomen as from a rock in the desert. During this intense wait her face presses close to his, until suddenly she feels as if her half-open mouth were lying caressingly on his cheekbone, as if he suddenly felt a sharp jet of saliva at his ear, shooting into the hair behind his ear, the little flood that precedes vomiting. . . . At the same moment a couple of rapid squirts tinkle on to the enamel down below. But it is not yet the breakthrough, not yet freedom. 'Wait,' says Grit at his ear. Bekker uncrosses his legs and holds Grit somewhat more securely and tenderly.

Waiting. Scratching and scraping. The body is rock, the body is closed up, language is closed up. Sedimentation and dislocation. One of many of the earth's crusts. But beneath our hesitant dry speech there must be a Great River. . . . In the municipal park a young, ugly woman goes walking, stinking and ashen-pale. Stinks out in the open air and no fresh breeze dispels the pungent stench. No longer wipes herself, just squats where she happens to be living and shits and pisses behind the filthy rag of her long shift-dress, which she never takes off. Bloated with eating rubbish, two fat warts next to each other on her cheek, round them violet veins, long hair like the Lorelei, down to her behind, matted and caked, dragged through Coke, oil and vomit so that it hangs stiff, as if glued, like a squashed mat at her back, decked out with rubbish of all kinds, matches, paperclips, bottle-tops, threads, nut-shells, chewing-gum, motley filth from the corners she generally lies and sleeps in, just as others put flowers or slides in their hair. In her wild unkemptness this woman has attained a certain perfection and seems to be wanting to say to us all: let it alone, be a shit-house yourself. But why then does she still hurry about among the trees in the park, among us, show herself so publicly in town, stinking her aggressive way towards us, particularly on summer days when we go walking in the park with the children, who promptly bawl like stuck pigs every time they so much as catch a distant glimpse of the stinking fairy? Ah, she wants to live, join in, needs to get about, hunt for her food and sun herself now and then on a bench as well, and drink from the little fountains that splash from the stone columns here. In town she can always get by more easily on kitchen remnants, charity and thieving than in the forests of the Eifel or the Schwäbische Alb. She has a taste for living among others yet without them. She simply wants to play with shit again and not be bothered. Just as some like to be tormented and have the daylights beaten out of their souls, or others greedily build houses. She takes a long look at her holed cardigan lying beside her on the bench. Looks cunningly at the rag and, with those wild eyes of hers, seems to be lying in wait for a creature that could move and decide to give her the slip. Cautiously she positions her hand over the jacket as if she meant to catch a fish from out of the rapids, and then with lightning speed she grabs. . . .

Are things any better among the owners of the world, with their sensitivity and body-care? Do we not find there too, more and more, the selfsame sickness of suddenly turning childish, in the midst of a dazzling rise? In the hall of her house, the Villa Sirius (designed by herself), covered all around with cool aluminium, stands a woman with her two daughters— the boss of more than fifty architects, draughtsmen, designers. Black hair cut short, emphasizing her narrow, longish head as one that is clear and gets its way. The smaller of the daughters talks sensibly to her mother, accepts advice as to how she should lay out a bed in the garden for tulips and one for anemones, while at the same time her sister, aged nineteen, with a school-leaving average grade of 1.6, snuggles into her mother's right arm and in an almost imbecile way, with a dull, distant backward look in her eyes, chews at her naked breast. The lady of the house has pulled up her pullover above her right breast and, as though it were the most common of customs, has left it to her older daughter. Without paying attention to this she goes on instructing the little one, who already apes her mother in a precocious manner and parrots everything she says. The collapse of the model pupil, the great jolt, came after the radiant 1.6-victory of her school-leaving certificate, which was in fact a victory of total destruction won by ambition, haste, restriction and the future over youth, maturing, dawdling, and first love. . . .

Grit is tormented by deceptive nervous irritations. Evidently the operation has caused an upset in the fibres, her urge to urinate is constantly strong but there is no relief. Through all that long wait, all that was added was a little snorting fart, which she smothered with a simultaneous sigh. 'Put me down again . . . On the other side.' As he lifts and supports her again, the night-dress slides high up and is caught on the thick dressing plastered on her back, and inadvertently

[104]

the matted, tangled hair between her legs, pressed together into a goatee, appears, now a place dedicated to pain, paralysis and sexless sickness alone, and for a fraction of a second a scrap of that early undisciplined dream of glimpsing beyond the boarded-up end of the world flashes through Bekker's head. 'Did you see the dressing on the wound?' asks Grit. Now she is lying on her left side and reaches herself paper handkerchiefs from the bedside table to dry her eyes and nose. 'Enormous, isn't it?' Bekker, awkward as ever before this sick child, answers, with as much thoughtlessness as caution: 'Yes. They must have made a long incision to get at it better. . .'. He notices his blunder even before he has finished speaking and feels like biting his tongue. Because there is nothing on account of which the girl feels sorrier for herself than the long scar which she may well have on her back. Hardly surprising that this comfortless comment is only followed by a growling 'Hm'. Bekker tries to get out of the embarrassment by beginning to report on his talk with the assistant director. But she interrupts him immediately and gives vent to her feelings about the man, whom she doesn't trust an inch, and considers a regular bringer of ill fortune. That doctor! And such dark glasses! (That is true. Bekker was bothered by it too, though other things bothered him more.) You'd sooner conceal your suffering from a doctor like that than reveal it to him. Has her father ever been treated by a doctor who couldn't look him straight in the eye? It's difficult enough in any case to spill out details to a stranger in that way . . . and then those glasses! That unflinching scrutiny from out of the dark. She has her own ideas about the openness towards people a doctor must have, she says, and the patient has a right to a candid face. . . . Well, they mustn't go on talking about this man—she doesn't want to hear his advice and warnings. One thing, though: her aversion to the assistant director and her scolding seem veritably to strengthen her, in the process she becomes positively lively and babbles away without restraint.

New Year's Eve in the hospital. Grit has given in after all now and has remained in the ward longer than absolutely necessary, for observation. After diligent exercising with the physiotherapist she is soon sufficiently recovered to go to the toilet alone and walk about in the corridor. The most dangerous complaint, the formation of residual urine, has not yet improved in the slightest. At midnight, when the old year ends, when the citizens all around set the lights dancing, Bekker and Grit, above it all, watch from the ninth floor of the clinic the dazzle and fall of a thousand flashes, balls, sheaves of fire, like a vast, joint, completely disorderly composition, sent up high from so many individual houses and estates and up there nonetheless a pattern created by them all, an organism of skipping joy above the town.

Not long after the fireworks have subsided, after the light New Year kiss she plants on her father's mouth, Grit falls on the spot into a deep sleep. A little champagne, and perhaps also Bekker's unaccustomed and unusually funny tales of the old officer, of his home-made Catherine wheels, thunderclaps and rockets, were just about able to keep her awake till midnight. Once she even grew positively high-spirited, with her pert crinkles under her eyes, and declared that she really did become somewhat restless now and then . . . Restless? Well, she meant a little eager for some loving, to put it bluntly: randy. No doubt ever since Joseph has been visiting her more frequently these last few days she may for the first time be feeling fully what she's missing once more. Her father stands a while longer at the window and tries to collect himself for the New Year, but he can't manage to meditate on what is to come or even to find anything worth planning for in the time ahead.

Then he packs up the remains of the cold buffet food that he had hastily obtained from a hotel kitchen late that afternoon without knowing that Grit cannot stand glazed titbits of this kind. He leaves the rubbish and the uneaten dainties with the nurses on night duty. Joseph, by contrast, had of course brought the right thing with him. A heap of oranges and giant

South African grapes. She sucked the latter ravenously. Joseph, once dismissed, has in the meantime gently rolled back. This ingenuous smiler you can never offend, in his jacket covered with peace-flowers, has turned out particularly reliable and helpful, and has taken over all the duties of the travel office, as far as he's been able. It is thanks to him that the agency hasn't had to close and there have been no major losses. He also has the knack of getting close to Grit without crowding her or renewing previous claims. A strangely painless and stretchable fabric of letting-go and keeping-hold contains these two, and Bekker is not mistaken in thinking that Joseph, who has inconspicuously offered so much support, aptitude, independence, will very soon be rediscovered by Grit in the most satisfactory way. You can't help noticing that the good-natured warmth she shows towards him now, as long as she still lies incapacitated on her sick-bed before him, could readily and very quickly be transformed into pure body-heat. Although, mind you, the lad has meanwhile been carrying on—admittedly in the background—with an unchanged averageness, with the selfsame qualities which, taken together and seen by the light of day, had already led once before to that deadly, agreeable boredom from which Grit needed at all costs to flee some months ago. By now they are again getting on splendidly by means of platitudes, and Grit seems to listen to him with a regular relief, his even empty phrases, these tones of his that tell of today or at least a very recent yesterday. Bekker suddenly realizes how very much his age, his acting old, his stammering, the thousand unhappy little aspirations of the spirit, must have burdened and overtaxed his child. With that quite special glow in the eyes, which in love is used only for welcoming one returning home, and with that smile—of old familiar things inducing shyness—she has taken a look at Joseph again, and more than once her gaze slid down to the bunch his testicles make in the wine-red velvet trousers. Reflectively she seemed to be wondering if adventure might not in fact lie deep down in security, if desire might not be concealed in accustomed ways, if you only searched properly and with determination.

Nevertheless, the earlier bond between the two of them is not simply restored. Individual encounters are as far as it goes. It is not Joseph but her father who is allowed to move into the flat in the Flämische Strasse with Grit once again, after her discharge from hospital. There he has his hands full for the first few days, with help and duties of every kind to fulfil, cooking, cleaning, shopping, washing. . . . Almost too much to cope with for a man who is inexperienced in housework and indeed has long lacked occupation of any kind, who now, startled out of his gloomy brooding, flaps about the flat with a forget-fulness to match his eagerness to serve. At first Grit is still obliged to spend most of the day in bed. She is very quickly fatigued by movement; bending or carrying things are not yet possible for her. Thus Bekker is now in sole charge of the household and deals with errands outside the house too, following her instructions. Yet all too often he, who believes in disorder and is permeated with it, finds her eyes are fixed on him steadily, even with disgust, when he gets up to something which, as Grit expresses it, a woman just can't bear to look at. Indeed, she soon finds it no longer funny or irritating but a painful annoyance when Bekker, say, clatters the plastic mouth of the vacuum cleaner across the bathroom tiles—the way he does it, it is like the grating of a knife-blade in a jam-jar. Things are brought into contact that do not go together. What are rusks doing in the toaster? And you don't set down the egg-timer next to a naked gas-flame! In a nervous, wild fashion Bekker presses on with his housekeeping, and in doing so gets further and further, in Grit's eyes, into a realm where use and meaning are stripped of sense and purpose, does everything at once, as diligently and no less vainly than if you were to polish your one-mark coins with Sidolin every day or dust down the cleaning-rag with a clothes-brush.

'Don't wipe like that!' Grit cries from her bed, revolted,

observing through the gap of the door her father at the bathroom mirror, the way he stands there, legs splayed out, his behind wobbling, avidly scrubbing like crazy at dried-on splashes of toothpaste. 'That looks positively indecent, the way you do it! . . . Really unpleasant!' Her father pauses, leaves the mirror, bends and begins to wipe out the wash-basin with a round, lazy movement, clearly feeling significantly less for it. Where does all the forcefulness and avidity in his clumsy hands come from? Whence all at once do these hands get such life—like a sex-murderer's? It all means something, doesn't it? Grit does not know why she nurses so profound a distaste for the activities of her father. Once, though, when he anxiously holds a colossal tax-office demand for back payments in his hand and reads it out, she looks him firmly and disdainfully in the eye and declares, without in any way commenting on the matter itself: 'He who is at odds with himself attracts disaster because he himself *is* a disaster.' Says it in a loaded and knife-edge tone and henceforth repeats this successful dictum on every apt and inapt occasion.

Her irritable defensiveness and the sudden thrust at her father alternate these days with conditions of profound downheartedness and enfeeblement, in which she seeks refuge with him and is grateful to have him near. For one thing, the great disappointment at the failure of her treatment remains, at the basic fruitlessness of her stay in the clinic and her operation—up till now there has not been a trace of improvement, least of all concerning the awful malfunctioning of the bladder muscles (rather, her numb left calf tends to tug and twitch, as if life were slowly creeping up in it), so that, exactly as before the operation, she is dependent on powerful medicines, general antibiotics that produce a persistent nausea and exhaustion of the entire circulatory system. For another thing, there is the cheerless certainty that a disease, probably not one that endangers life but quite likely one that can never be cured either, is lodged in her back, like dry rot in roof-beams, constantly threatening her in some uncertain way. Last but not least, the spiritual irritation persists after such an operation, which went, as it were, to the very marrow, the centre of fears, however insignificant it may have been in a surgical sense. All of this taken together leads to Grit's going for the first time through a deeper exhaustion of her simple and robust consciousness. At night especially, in a half-slumber, the soft misgrowth in her back, which her thoughts are incessantly touching, is inflated to monstrous dimensions, and nameless fear then creates the very same horrific image, every time, of a pregnancy in which the fruit of evil is carried in numerous tiny freaks. Scuttling embryos, in the form of animals or cripples, loathsome visions of birth and abortion beset her. And every time there appears as well the young male nurse with his crafty grin, presumably the man she made out first, in a blur, once the far too heavy anaesthetic began to wear off, and who now appears as the deranged father of her verminous child. He comes to her with a harrying grimace, with a hideous seriousness, and instructs her in that sleight of hand by means of which you 'nowadays' dispose of a child once it has been brought into the world, 'inconspicuously': you hollow out a large pumpkin, shove the new-born child into it, close the pumpkin and stick it carefully shut, take it to the market and leave it there among the many other pumpkins. Another time he performs another didactic play, and, with two paring knives, cuts a baby out of the breast of a naked tailor's dummy with a male upper half. If she starts up out of such nightmares, things are no less haunted in her waking: then she hears her father sleeping in the next room, separated from her by a thin partition wall only, his even and monotonous puffing like that of one condemned to spend damnation's eternity doing the breast-stroke. So she has now made a nightmare of her protector, by letting his bed come far too close to her own. 'Soon he'll have to go back to the far end of the flat,' she thinks. And: 'He'll have to move out of the flat altogether soon. . .'.

On the other hand it is her father who gets woken in the middle of the night by a scream or groan. Then he goes across to her room, switches on the bedside light, and raises her restless head from the pillow in both hands. At once she sits bolt upright, clings to his shoulder and gives a first-hand report from the place of horror. . . . She came across some old letters just now and there was something terrible among them. A cellophane envelope, completely transparent, with all the white eaten away. A worm, a kind of black, feathered worm, no, a tiny, agile moray eel with pointed teeth, that scurried about in the envelope, in a heap of pitch-black, flimsy threads of paper, and that was its excrement, the discharged white. She or it had eaten all the white from the paper in the still unopened letter, over a sojourn of years. . . . 'But that,' exclaims Grit, interpreting the dream almost indignantly, 'but that is just like a child, an unborn life, that cannot get out!' Thus her dreams keep on running on the spot, as it were, the material is almost always similar, brief and deathless as a scrap of music when the needle of the record-player cannot pass a scratch and never reaches the next groove. And just as the finished idea or prophecy originates in the senseless circling of a fragment, so she in the end presumes her dream's happenings, involving mother and child and time and again the male nurse, to be incontestably true. For how should he not have easily got at her, how should he not have taken easy advantage of the opportunity, when she lay under the anaesthetic still and noticed nothing? Further, all the nausea, and in general a creeping feeling of finding herself different. That's settled, then: she is pregnant, raped by this unpleasant character in health sandals and white hospital coat. . . .

To push this crazy notion even further, her father counters that her suspicion need not be restricted to the poor male nurse alone. Why should not Manstett, the chief, be considered too, even the assistant director, and indeed—if you're going to have such dark fantasies—why not himself, her father himself? 'Who?' asks Grit, and looks at him maliciously.

'You hardly recognized me at all the first time I came to visit you,' her father says, and almost squints with cunning and eagerness.

'What first visit? What are you talking about? Ah, I can't

[111]

stand it when you pull such a screwed-up face. Go now. As of tomorrow you won't be sleeping in the next room any more.'

Her father has to take a little rubber container with Grit's urine to the chemist's for a pregnancy test. The result, as was to be expected, is negative. But strangely she reacts in a downcast manner, rather than with relief. 'Most things don't happen in life,' she says, and folds the chemist's bill smaller and smaller, 'not to me at any rate.'

Then she allocates a back room to her father, more of a closet than a room, next to the bathroom and with only a narrow window giving on to the back area. There he is to sleep and spend his evenings too; he is not to show up too much in the front rooms in the evenings.

In the following week Grit has again regained her strength sufficiently to work half-days at least in the travel agency. This and that has remained unattended to after all. In particular, Joseph has not always had a happy hand with the correspondence. You have to deal firmly with travel companies at times. What is more, the first wave of summer bookings is already well under way, and the regular customers want Grit herself, showing the way to the distant places with grace, just as she does at this time every year.

As long as he is alone the whole flat is at her father's disposal, with the exception of Grit's bedroom. Recently she has been keeping this locked. From time to time she brings Joseph with her in the evenings and the two of them watch something on television.

Bekker goes about the town again now, night after night, gathering about him in the pubs a circle of those who are partly his friends and partly just smile at him, those who listen to him, to whom he spouts forth his fragmented stories and visions just as soon as he has drunk enough and has got into the mood. He is far less inhibited now, he makes a public show of himself, conspicuously makes himself known, in fact he even tells his stories for money. For to have his glass filled up again

[112]

and again with good cognac he needs more than the dole will pay out. Hence in this new, sociable phase of his addiction to the town he soon becomes a pub character at the centre of hooting attention, nicknamed the Stammerer and introducing himself as such before tossing out his unpolished monologues. These are listened to with a muted responsiveness by the young and uninformed in particular, students and renegades from all scenes and sects, and are requested again and again as a new kind of popular poetry or cabaret. But it is also evident that many of his fantasies are only slightly accessible to the audience, and only when he is really able to get out of himself and an urgent utterance pours forth do the people listen not solely on account of this powerful, unusual phenomenon, this undaunted number. Then they suddenly have a hard, dark battering of crows' wings about their heads, only spoken words, and they do not laugh at it. Such an offering cannot be repeated pub after pub. Often enough it has a hollow effect, inconsequential, external, and affects no one, an embarrassing programme. Seeing One Human Being caused him to see visions. They are not suitable for marketing, for handing on to countless others. This notwithstanding, he allows himself to be talked into it when his drinking companion Ludwig, a night-show radio editor with a fussy concern for Brokdorf, invites him to play the midnight fool, to talk away frankly for half an hour for a good fee in his studio, in the soundproof booth, live. In this broadcast, where everything and anything is to be presented lightly in a mixed-up manner and the listener is not meant to distinguish what is serious and what a parody, Bekker is introduced by Ludwig, who behaves in an artificially coarse and cheeky way at the microphone, as 'one of the last ventriloquists in the land of liars, of mouths that hang open and mouths that have been shut'.

Then Bekker is given a signal and begins to speak up in a whisper. He starts with a tender invocation of the old officer; at first he avails himself of the radio's unbounded air-waves to get in touch with the soul of one who is dead. Everything that occurs to him has to do with the officer, whose goodness and wickedness, whose language and nonsense, he says, follow him to this very day, so that he frequently already thinks that during his lifetime he is offering up nothing but the low, striving repetition of a speech he's done without. This takes a good while and over behind the pane the editor pulls a long, sullen face. 'Above all, being old,' says Bekker, addressing the microphone personally, 'is a genuine essence of being. And suddenly. With shock one follows the next beyond, and they're old. Other people are no longer inclined to consider old people as if they could find anything in them. They want nothing from them. You have to put up with it. Even your own dreams have locked you out. But if at night there's just the murmur of a little traffic in the distance, you're reassured. These people are busy, they're driving, they don't love each other. As long as something is driving outside, an engine is running, everything passes. In the house next door an old man has sealed up his letterbox slit with masses of broad sellotape, and a note is attached, on which is written: Hans Wöllner. Letters, newspapers, circulars. Nothing else! . . . That is a first step.'

But then, suddenly, a few hoarse cries break forth, summons to assassinate the bosses and the powerful at every level, and there follows a loud, indefinable fatherlandish howl, so that even Ludwig, who is out for gimmicks and scandal, shifts the tone controls at the desk and drowns out his droning night-watchman with fade-ins of old hits and a comic *mélange* of Bundestag speeches edited together.

Bekker notices none of this and continues talking indefatigably. Now, in the style of eye-witness reports, he is representing a stupendous vision of the new migrations of nations, giving an account of the Great Crusades from the south, in the course of which millions of the starving from all over the world invade our country, weak in faith and under-populated, to relieve their need and keep us old folk in tutelage. In the end he cannot resist directing a completely personal address of hatred at his bosom enemy, Zachler, the worst swine in the world: when he opens his mouth the coffin of the German Wehrmacht opens! . . . But by then he has long been off the air.

After his radio appearance Bekker hops about the streets for a long time, still involved with a violent murmuring in his speech, which pursues him like a cloud of gnats and which he again and again tries to harness towards an attractive ending. Once he stops still in an empty pedestrian subway and calls about him: 'That's it! That's it! I have spoken. . . . I'm through!' But hardly has he gone two paces further than he already continues: 'Oh damn it. Nothing spoken. Oral schmoral. Just so much singsong. I'm a singer and a good whack of the silent majority on top of it. You should hear me—but not *you* you, Zachler, and your Nature!'

On the steps of the subway a pack of Pakistanis come towards him, and he steps in their way with a friendly bow and asks if he can be of assistance. The men, nearly a dozen of them, most of them in thin nylon coats and colourful pullovers, look uncomprehendingly at him, turn past him right and left and leave him standing.

They saunter at a moderate pace like tourists on the first evening at their journey's destination, and yet prefer to keep their attention fixed within the group, just themselves closed off against strangers and everything unfamiliar. A little troop of the displaced and abandoned, such as you come across more frequently in town nowadays. They have sold themselves to a slave-trader in their home countries, as manpower for Germany, and are now made to realize that in the promised land they are neither needed nor even tolerated, and get neither employment nor a residence permit. Mute and dazed they wander through the town, begin dully to suspect what a wicked swindle, what a monstrous deception it is that they have fallen victim to. Bekker runs after the men and, when he has caught up with them, saunters along with the pack, as if attracted by these aimless walkers from the East. After a while he speaks to a very young lad who is walking beside him: 'Work? . . . You

[115]

want a job?"* The lad does not look at him, but another man, who is walking in front of him, turns, and all the rest remain standing too. Yes, says the man, quietly and warily, almost combat-ready. Bekker, with over-zealousness in his eyes and hands, stands before the group and explains in English that he can procure them work, that he is able to get them good, well-paid work, work and papers, job—papers—job! He laughs once, vehemently, into the air, filled with happiness by the ease of this new-found role of his, as saviour of man. If they will only follow him, he says, and takes his place at the head of the Pakistanis, who now behind his back chatter on in their native tongue and promptly become somewhat silly too, for they have instantly rediscovered trust in their good fortune. Just like their pace, which grows faster and gains a direction and a goal, their heads are raised as well and they notice the way they are going, look into display windows and back-streets, just as you pay extra special attention when you first walk to a new place of work, since from every shop, every traffic light, your whole future of walking along here every day and soon without any awareness at all confronts you. Bekker addresses himself to the spokesman and actual leader of the group and repeats that it is of importance to him, is a personal satisfaction to him, to be able to help them, the Pakistanis, to be able to get them work, for it is he himself who has work to give and is thus in a position to enable these displaced people to stay legally. He leads them by way of crooked side-streets to an area of factories and warehouses and at last assembles them in the courtyard of an old brick building in front of a high, locked iron gate. 'Here work'. On the wall next to the gate a brass plaque is fixed on which there stands in fat, prominent block letters: 'Bekker & Klapproth, Haulage Contractors. Storage Depot'. He points to the name Bekker and places his hand on his breast: 'That's me. That's me.' He steps aside and the strangers stare at the sign as if at a memorial tablet. 'Okay? I

* Here and in the following pages, in the original text, Bekker speaks mainly in English when addressing the Pakistanis (translator's note).

am the owner. You can work here. I need some good store-workers. You come tomorrow morning, okay?' These words are taken in and expounded among the Pakistanis with liveliness, with a suddenly unrestrained loudness. Some of them are visibly seized by impatience and would clearly like to get behind the rust–red gate, right away, at least take a look behind it. But it seems questions are being asked too. Bekker takes out his wallet and beckons the leader over to him. He shows him his identity card, requests him to compare the name Bekker on the sign and on the paper, letter by letter. After the leader has done this he hands on the identity card to one of his friends, without however showing him what he is to examine. So the identity card goes the rounds and each of the men compares the passport photo with Bekker's actual face, like a frontier guard. Obsessed and reckless, as if it were a question this evening of nothing less than his own survival, Bekker sues for the trust of these men, would like to get in among them, really snuggle in among these strangers, into the blue–black hollow of this pack of people turned, listening, to him. The Pakistanis, however, remain on the whole reserved, shy, unwarmed. They are completely uninterested in an exchange of human feelings of well-being, but are solely interested in that treasure there beyond the gate, which back home they had been promised they would find at the end of the long trip, and to the palpable proximity of which exactly the right German has now led them at the right moment. They accept it as if it were as they expected, as if it were as ordered and paid for.

'Tomorrow morning, eight o'clock. Okay?' The men nod. They seem to be unsuspicious of Bekker and the promises he has given as the boss of a transport business. Then he bids them follow him again and takes them a number of blocks further to his favourite pub, the Baerwaltklause, and there, jovial and contented, like the German trainer at the head of an oriental football team, makes his entry with his pack. He leaves the hundred or so marks of his radio fee with the innkeeper and shows him with big gestures what kind of

[117]

massive spread he wants and with what ample, typically German fare he wants to see it decked out for his guests. When he invites them to a first round, though, he is disappointed. None of the men will be induced to drink cognac with him or even the slightest drop of any kind of alcohol. At table it is Bekker alone, then, who tirelessly provides the entertainment, even if at first it consists only in his trying to learn and use the name of every one of them round the table and occasioning a lot of sociable laughter, even from the stoniest faces, with the comical mispronunciations usual in such situations. Later he gives them a full account of the rise and present-day significance of his transport business, describes the making of a success, from lorry-driver to boss, leaves nothing out, like a spy who has fully mastered his cover story, not his wife, or child, or partner Klapproth, holidays, customs dues, wages, energy problems. With utter inevitability he ends up talking about his arch-enemy too, Zachler, the world's dirtiest pig, who makes his appearance in this other life as the unscrupulous competitor with a dishonest price tariff.

Meanwhile Bekker has knocked back half a litre of cognac or more, which at the outset made the torrent of his speech all the more powerful and lent to his English an ever stronger German accent. Up to the moment when, in one single, clumsy slide, he suddenly becomes so totally drunk that the crests of the waves of intoxication splash together over him and he is no longer capable of speaking distinctly, far less of standing upright on his legs. The Pakistanis sit about somewhat uneasy, all of them silent in their places, and listen to this mindless, stupidly babbling man, who is after all supposed to be their boss; they listen but prefer not to look, with a kind of pious embarrassment, much as the uninitiated might behave next to a spitting shaman having a seizure. Every one of them fixes his gaze on his *vis-à-vis* and only in response to direct addresses do they look down, shyly, out of the corners of their eyes, to see how the boss, doubled over the table edge, is conducting himself. Now, in fact, they seem secretly to be waiting for him to fall asleep, so that they can get away unnoticed. But Bekker straightens up and groans, with his eyes wide open with fear: 'Don't leave me alone! Just don't leave me alone!' The Pakistanis' spokesman, however, explains carefully that it is already very late in the night and they all really ought to get back to their pension.

'Take me with you!' cries Bekker. 'I come with you, take me along!' He leaps up from his chair and immediately slumps down sideways as if pulled down by the earth. Some of the men spring to his assistance and try to raise him to his feet again, but he won't stay standing and they have to support him under the arms. He talks all manner of incomprehensible stuff. But out of the thick mumbling the sounds of a childish pleading repeatedly come through, which must be comprehensible to anyone, even the most foreign of strangers, as much as a smile or a scream. And once more, no doubt with his last strength, he becomes lucid and distinct, and orders softly: 'Take me along.'

Although the men—up till then a squad united in their decisions—now suddenly argue about whether they can take Bekker with them or even want to do so, they begin by carrying him lengthwise out of the pub.

Since he refuses to creep into a taxi, or far more, when one stops and the door is already open, clings to the neck of his bearers with strangling strength, the leader of the group steps in and ends the wrangle with a loud word of command. He decrees that Bekker is not to be left to his fate but carried on. Now they continue to bear him along without any grumbling, and all of them seem instantly to be of one opinion. Bekker, horizontal under the heavens, breathes happily out and behind his closed eyelids rolls the balls of his eyes, once, gratefully. In this way he enjoys the help he is given as others enjoy sunbathing.

In the cleared-out breakfast-room of a little, dirty pension run by two Turks, some twenty sleeping Pakistanis are already lying on the floor. They have laid out makeshift beds for themselves with blankets and articles of clothing, crowded close to each other, and recycle choking air, a mixture of pungent vapours from remainders of food in plastic bags, from bodies and clammy clothing, an intolerable stench; for Bekker, however, who snuffles at foreignness like an enthusiast ecstatically sniffing mushroom-fluid, this means access to the longed-for atmosphere of a completely different world, skin and food. The latecomers shove in among their sleeping comrades, stretch out on the coats and pullovers. Bekker is laid down next to their leader, who pushes an embroidered cushion from an office chair under his head. 'Thank you, thank you,' murmurs Bekker, and reaches for the solicitous hand, which, however, pulls back from him hard and shy. He lies awake on the back of his head for a short, happy review of the position, tries to savour to the full his asylum, the protection of the dorm as well as the remoteness of his own person, till all his certainty deserts him and his face slips on to the cushion, which stinks of dog-pelt and anus.

Toward morning he is evicted from his slumbers by a bitter dream, a most inward expulsion from sleep. Without properly knowing what he is doing or what he intends, he rouses himself and creeps out of the room on all fours. In the hall he pulls himself upright by the banister and totters unsteadily down to the exit. He leaves the pension. Outside it is still dark and quiet. A damp cold assails him, he coughs and expectorates. Ahead of him the crossroads and a solitary lit-up window on the other side flicker in his drunken head like a film shortly before it tears.

His whole body trembling, he stumbles across the road. The light is the light of a snack stall which is already serving. It is situated next to a bus station. There Bekker orders his first cognac of the morning. He is soothed by listening to the bus drivers, who have just received the news of the death of a colleague who had a heart attack during the night. For this reason they are in no mood for jokes. The death of a person quite unknown to him weaves towards him through the quiet, stunned talk of the men, touches him and lifts him like a wave

[120]

that would bear a man who is stranded back out to the open human sea. But then he goes to the telephone and dials the police. He identifies himself as the landlord of the 'Utah' pension, Utah like the American federal state, at the corner of the Oranienstrasse and Fichtenbergstrasse, and claims to have thirty-five illegal Pakistani immigrants in his rooms, whom his wife inadvertently took in without his knowledge and who now steadfastly refuse to quit his house again. But he knows that these poor devils ought to be deported and that he cannot keep them on his premises any longer. So he is requesting police help . . . Afterwards he takes a second cognac and then goes back to the pension, the street door of which he had left on the latch on leaving. He sneaks up to the dorm and lies down in his place again amid the sleeping men.

Half an hour later two police vans pull up outside. The proprietors are summoned down by the bell and try to refuse the officers admission by denying that they rang them at all. At the same time the Turks are far too excited to act stupid for long enough, and fidgety denial does not in the long run make the anonymous informant's denunciation any less credible.

So the policemen turn up a little later in the Pakistanis' dorm, not heavily armed, it is true, but still in overdone strength, some six or eight men, among them some very young ones, with gangling movements and hair that curls over the edges of their caps, so that it looks as if an immature lad like that will split his uniform apart with his growth. The Pakistanis are woken with loud battering at the door, which is in any case open, and without any prior explanation or inspection of papers are ordered to pack up their things and get ready for transport to the foreign section. Most of them, in particular those who did not make Bekker's acquaintance the previous evening, willingly and promptly do what is required of them. Obviously they have for a long time been expecting nothing else but to be discovered one day in this manner and taken away. They give no sign at all of surprise or of any rebelliousness. After so many rebuffs and such a long, vain quest they must see the officers more or less as travel escorts, who will now, at last, be responsible for their free passage home. Bekker alone is obliged to produce identification. He is particularly roughly treated. No doubt they suspect that in him they have caught an agent, a German middleman in what the newspapers always call the filthy, villainous slave-trade. Just as he is still maintaining that he happens to be here merely because he is a personal friend of a group of these men and, by way of proof, is reciting some of the names he still retains from the night before, enunciating them in an almost caressing way: Ghulam, Fakhar, Ifran, Nalem, Quaissar . . . , he is bawled out by one of the junior officers, who suddenly and from the very depths of his own heart gives vent to a tremendous indignation at that human filth which the slave-trader represents for him. The men whose names Bekker mentioned look across at him for a last time, one after the other, to see if anything else will come or can be expected from him, their confused master. When this does not happen, and, far more, they observe that he is handled even more contemptuously by the representatives of the state than they themselves, they no longer pay any attention to him and cut him with their looks.

Even on the drive to the police-station, and later, when he is being questioned, good and proper, Bekker lapses into a mulish pensiveness, into a melancholy as sovereign as it is bottomless. His deed, affection and the betrayal of affection, is metamorphosed for him into a profound and abstract event that should never be talked about. So he only answers questions concerning his person, and replies to any suggestion of a criminal side to his relationship with the Pakistanis with one sole impertinent word, uttered in an uncouth tone: 'Rubbish'. Since he is not permitted to get away with this indefinitely—since the officers are for their part provoked by it to embody the power of the Law with greater insolence— Bekker, after one incident, a gross threat of imprisonment, becomes suddenly annoyed and demands to speak to his daughter at home, so that she can get him a lawyer. Thus he telephones Grit and explains what has happened to him, in a few, unusually precise and definite words, so that she has no opportunity to groan, reproach him or enquire after the meaning of his actions. He asks her to get in touch with Bruno Stöss, his former and only intimate friend at the Institute, for he can recall his getting him an excellent lawyer once before in another matter. Grit answers with composure, almost as if it were a routine affair, instructs her father to refuse to make a statement, to reject every accusation, and to restrain his fantasy, so that he does not thoughtlessly incriminate himself . . .

Barely an hour later Bekker is released from custody. Yet without any lawyer having intervened. Grit had done what she had been asked to do, but Bruno Stöss at the Institute had taken a different course at his own discretion, had not retained a lawyer, since he thought he knew how this affair could be dealt with in a less complicated way. He had informed Zachler. In that state of agitation in which one would like to bring together and reconcile two people for both of whom one has an undying love and who nevertheless are each other's sworn enemies he had run to the boss and asked him to use his influence on Bekker's behalf. He had simply sensed that here was the chance, perhaps the last, to re-unite the master with his 'talented hound', as Zachler had at one time liked to call him; and Bekker himself, he believed, would undoubtedly be moved by the boss's intercession to pull himself together at last and return to the Institute before it was once and for all too late and his self-dismembering left only a useless idiot behind, a wreck in mind and soul. Zachler reached for the receiver without hesitation—yet so quickly, in fact, that not the slightest sign of any inner emotion could be perceived in him, nothing of his true feelings concerning Bekker, whether he still wanted the latter's return (as he had once confessed in secret some weeks previously) or whether this man who was constantly trying to make war on him had become of utter indifference to him now that he was down at the bottom and defeated. So Zachler had himself put through to the head of the foreign section, a civil servant he was well acquainted with, and, speaking aloof and quickly, as is his way, declared that one of his employees, Bekker, was conducting research into the illegal job market on behalf of the Institute, that such an undertaking demanded an undercover approach by the very nature of the business, and that, in order to throw light on so-called dark statistics, the investigator must operate in the protection of darkness himself, as it were. . . .

Zachler gave Bekker a good character. It cost him little effort to get Bekker, this soldier who has gone astray and cannot find his way back to the battle, free again.

That evening Bekker returns somewhat cringing and intimidated. He has not found out whose hand it was that protected him, nor is he interested in finding out. It is less the police detention that occupies him than, solely and incessantly, the adventure of his radio talk and—following upon it in some inconceivable way—the Pakistani wanderings and his betrayal of affection.

The rebellious speaker has now slumped. All that he can get out now is a thin, sad murmuring. The transfixed seer has cracked. He has nothing with which to counter Grit's harsh, cool gaze. He looks aside with a somewhat insulted mien, like the little boy who, after a major misdemeanour, has been slapped on the back of his head and responds with the counter-punishment of an aloof expression of grief: a pity about us, mum. . . . Yet in this way motherly feelings, not to mention feelings of guilt, cannot be aroused in Grit. Rather, she is after a heart-to-heart talk with him this evening. In the television room they sit across from each other in two wheeled leather armchairs. 'What are you doing?' Grit asks, giving up the attempt to understand. 'How is it to go on?' And: 'When will you finally go back to the Institute?' Her father continually shakes his head and just before he utters the first sound of a reply always thinks better of it again. With a sigh she reaches for her sewing and begins to darn the pocket lining of Bekker's traditional jacket. It is not until long after she has posed her last, now quite indifferent question—'What did you say at the

[124]

police-station, as to who you are? What on earth did you tell them?'—that from the other side a soft, continuous murmuring comes across, something with a waste, cast-off sound to it, as if things forgotten, things that had escaped his memory, were speaking of their own accord. . . . 'I couldn't speak before the State, you see. All I could do at the State was stand round speechless. Just twitch stupidly, like with Schmidt, the Latin teacher, always teachers before me, but I speak as if I was the swot in *tres faciunt collegium*, whichever three they are. I'm 42 now or even 42½, as big as my shoe size. Deep down and askew on kindly soles. The deed is done. Language, the nut, splits and splits and splits itself and others. Hundreds of thousands! No, Law, it's not you I'm forgetting. Law! you indeed read me. Read me out, my darling, out loud. For at the very bottom of the world, by the Lahn, deep and askew, there stands an apple-cutter, and at night he gathers our fruit that hangs forgotten by everyone. And his cap doesn't slip off his head, looking up in the moon-round crown of his tree. Greet each other, go on, you tree and you man, bowing, greet each other again! . . . At last. Nothing lovelier than growing old in a young democracy. Lip-smacking, taut trousers on the arse! and marasmus. Clever people, well-prepared. Only the destroyers are punished severely. Them of all people, the assassins! . . . The State's nonsense!—the State itself has little idea of what's right, except that it possesses a lot of know-how and is the creator of this perfumed garden-prison where we can all run about hither and thither and each of us may also climb up for a while on a column, a TV mast for all I care, and look down, after all, Simon Stylites was up there for 43 years. What is more, as I said, the State itself doesn't know what's right and really ought not to be against assassins, who are life itself, like all fission fungi. There's precious little fatherland left, calls itself punishment and discipline. The noose of lies twists and twists. Take no one's hand any more! The nation pricks up its ears. Clown's gear shrivels up. All my spokesmen are racketeers. . . . Dear Sir, a racketeer writes to me from far away, You are infantile. No visits! . . . My goodness! Bake

[125]

yourself rolls on your heated head or stool! . . . I spoke on the radio once, so what? All on my own in the middle of the night, when even Sir Recording Engineer nodded off benevolently. "Why on earth have you got yourself up so sprucely?" he asks me, "no one can see you!" Maybe, I say to him, but this evening is something special for me. I sat on my own for hours under the microphone's cross. But I didn't incite or scold anyone. And no one was inciting me either or scolding me. In town more or less everything is near and out the window. By the Lahn in those days you would have had to put a hundred kilometres behind you to get to the heart of the radios. And I wouldn't have been accepted because I was far too young. . . . In New York on 14th Street someone spoke to me who knew who Carl Schmitt is. Me happy. Fine, a ladies', okay, I'll go pee somewhere else. But to be barred from the premises for that? Goodness, but your heads are all bound up with anger, you exploiters of the rays. . . . You're not worth the snot of the song! All that can be done, damn it, is to stamp one's foot and lash out. And for all that, how good it would be to be subordinate for once with your Whole Heart to someone stronger and stronger in suffering . . . such as my tree there, the big one right there is My Chestnut. Could be it'll die off for grief at the death of its human comrade. We've been together long enough. My my, they tell me, making up to trees like that just simply isn't decent, you know! and they run that down for me too. I was only standing next to it alone. Couldn't give a light. And I burnt out, the glow faded, I charred, fragmented, fell apart. I'll see to it that they dye my ashes. Blond, as I was, a German.

I am probably old and outside there is almost nothing more. Summer, winter and their companions, yes, are still there. But that gives me little joy. Even now I'm already sighing under the too heavy wings of my lungs. Only the eyes, the eyes . . . the pair of them! A last real partnership. But otherwise? Man stands out unattractively on the globe. When the angel comes to clear us up, he'll fold those who're standing in the middle, the heads to the feet.'

In the course of the next few days Bekker sees to it that he only rarely appears before Grit and, if he in fact does so, he says nothing and immerses himself in the various tasks that he has allotted himself in the flat and kitchen. He carries out these tasks rather less conspicuously nowadays: quietly but without pause. In fact it looks as if, in this solitary, ceaseless management of the household, he were seeking to cancel out—as if it were a curse—what he has committed outside as a useless and offensive member of society. His ambition and pleasure consist in leaving nothing unattended to and thinking of everything in advance. In the middle of the night, as he has no alcohol to drink and can hardly sleep, it occurs to him how much Grit likes to have fresh nuts to hand, and that she just ran out of them while watching television. So he fetches the basket of nuts from the larder, a supply which is filled up every day, and sits by his table lamp to crack open equal quantities of walnuts, hazelnuts, peanuts and Brazil nuts and count them into separate heaps. Although he cracks each single nut as carefully as if a pearl might be concealed in it, the splitting of the shells with an old nutcracker does occasionally send a loud report through the night-time quiet. After a while there is a rattle at his closet and Grit is standing in the doorway, naked, sleepy, her eyes screwed-up. 'What are you doing?' she asks gruffly. Her father shows her and offers the pile of nuts in his cupped hands. 'You can hear that cracking all over the house! Stop it.' She turns away from the door and slams it behind her. Whish! The stiff, brisk breeze of a matron's uniform cuts the air. . . . Bekker tumbles all the kernels into a big glass bowl and turns them over till he has got precisely that jumbled mixture that is pleasing. A market without a soul about! he whispers, reading the nuts, a market without a soul about, a market deserted by everyone in broad daylight, with tables, stands full of fruit, eggs, poultry, money, cash registers and signs, but no dealers, no buyers . . . an abandoned wealth, of no use to anyone any more. . . . Oh, this door pulled open and such a flash that it stops my breath and here I sit, red-headed, and red-handed. Oh not the thumbscrew and collar of

[127]

visions! . . . A man under a glass cover, the cashier in his cabin. The newly-opened bank building with its many friendly plants, its fresh green, its ornate staircases, its sound-proofing, its high dark-tinted glass walls, its refined Renaissance music and its leather swings in front of little fountain basins for the clients to pass their time in the glass-roofed court. . . . The man has experienced no devotion, no foundation in his life, he does not know the positive yes of love. Now he cannot take his eyes off the girl who is standing in front of his cash-desk waiting for him to change three hundred marks into dollars for her. He looks into the strangely dilated, black pupils of the beautiful customer's eyes. It seems as if she would like to look everywhere. But her eyes move infinitely more slowly than any other human eyes and are interrupted by not even a single blink of her lashes. He cannot get enough of looking at that wide gaze waiting for his fingers. Abruptly he dreams of a sky-high ocean wave—spring-tide they used to say, before they'd seen the likes of it—rolling in from the horizon—towering upright like a giant cobra, putting everything in the shade—towards the land, smashing our cities and jamming the people high against the walls of houses, and bloody foam is lit by falling ceiling lights. . . . With the greatest despondency the cashier says: 'I don't want to alarm you but the notes you gave me aren't genuine. They're counterfeit.' He feels as if his voice were coming out of a tiny transistor right in front, hanging just behind his upper lip, so tiny does his own sound seem. The beautiful customer looks straight at him and then, infinitely slowly, returns her gaze to his fingers. No doubt about it: she is still waiting. She is waiting undaunted. She is silent. The monstrous thing he said does not move her. And now she even taps the long, pointed, matt-varnished nail of her right forefinger on the marble ledge before the cash-desk window, urging him on a little.

He wonders if she has not understood him. Surely she is a German, isn't she? And even if she isn't, even if she's Finnish or some even more remote citizen of the world, in response to such a statement about counterfeit money you'd at least expect her to ask or put on an enquiring expression. So why is she not asking anything? The employee has long not dared look up where the girl towers above him. Oh, he thinks, no doubt she is impertinently waiting for me to look at her and, happy and entranced by the sight of her, quietly act as if I hadn't realized the money is fake, and behave as befits fingers that pay out. But he refuses to repeat the statement about the counterfeit money. And the girl goes on waiting. If other customers were standing behind her waiting for this endless person to be dealt with, the pressure would increase to unearthly proportions and burst human consciousness asunder. But as luck would have it there is no one behind her. Now, as if in the grip of extreme boredom, she looks up and down the prettily appointed banking chambers. And I'll give her nothing! the cashier thinks, and will quite positively never look at her again, and I won't say it a second time, either. . . . So the lives of both of them remain arrested, till nothing, nothing whatsoever moves any more.

I have to get out of here! exclaims Bekker, and he hurls the bowl with the nuts from the table. I have to get out of here, whatever happens, right now!—as if he were a cockroach floundering in the outlet of the sink.

He runs out of the closet and into the forward part of the flat. He pulls open the door of Grit's bedroom and blurts out into the darkness: 'Why are you isolating me like this?! Why? I can't stand it any more. You shift my bed from the next room into that so terribly solitary room, right at the back of our flat, and I'm cut off from everything at the front. The niche, the closet behind the bathroom is practically a tomb, and you wake up there in the mornings feeling completely nailed up. You say my gasping and puffing in my sleep frightened you. Fair enough. The noises I make in my sleep may have got worse over the years. But I ask you: doesn't it sound like the panting cries for help of a cruelly gagged soul? That's how it seems to me. And no one can do anything about the puzzling depths and aloneness of sleep. Not even when they're closest. And if you knew on top of that how my head thrashes about to left and right on the pillow every morning, like a stuck animal in its death throes—'

Suddenly he falls silent. In the midst of his complaint his courage has all at once been exhausted. One moment rebellion, then in the same instant submission once again—he sneaks quietly back out of the darkness of the bedroom, without waiting for even a hint of an answer, and then he flees from the forward part of the flat. Before his eyes he sees Grit sitting bolt upright in bed, though he has not seen her at all, growing more and more awake till at last her eyes are gaping wide open . . .

For a while, when he was busy nursing Grit and thus really had to be of use, Bekker regained his stability and level-headedness, as sober and reliable as you expect a man to be in his early forties with normal professional and family ties. You could once again ask him for advice on all kinds of things, too, and he was in a position to master his experience and deliver a reasonable, collected speech.

Now, after the worry, all this is over again. With ever greater clarity the mask of the old man is now emerging from the tired, broad face, again the flickering of his spirit, strangely advanced in age, is increasing. The features of strength and of decay dominate one and the same face together, as in some unstable fabulous monster, now living in two times at once, now alternating between them, living out its life in the present and the future, manhood and senility at once. The matt, grey-blue eyes, wide and unwishing. The compulsive wandering of his gaze when Grit is talking to him, and everything, the most unimportant object, distracts him and diverts his attention from listening. His unkempt dark blond hair, slept-on and tangled, long since uncombed, spiky and wispy. The slack folds under his chin, the drinker's grooves under his eyes, the dry, flaky skin, the somewhat too short, turned-up nose like that of a Silenus, and yet above everything the broad, steep forehead, the front you can't creep up on, always well-defended. The right hand often reposing over the heart as if in expectation of a thump from in there, or maybe only to press the nipple nervously now and then. The bloated cheeks and the full, limp mouth, the lips that have something so soft about them, indeed softened, that reminds you of a roll dunked in coffee. His mouth forever half open, as if an immoderate cry had strained the muscles, his complexion so weak and pale, as if it had faded for good after an immoderate blanching—an abrupt, absolute loss of colour that no skin ever recovers from. Thus, as if through the most powerful rays of a storm, he has suddenly turned an old man and half an idiot, in the midst of his prime and just as—shortly before his fourth session there—he circles the Zachler Institute, the inescapable place of work.

Grit observes her father about the most bizarre business. For example, she finds him crouched on his knees on the floor combing the carpet fringe straight with the tips of his fingers: he is getting the TV room ready for her so that things at home will be in order when she comes in from work. Also disquieting is his constant nodding off, wherever he is sitting reading, and often he sticks to the newspaper all day long, needing to cross off the articles he has read so that he does not read them again and again. In such absentmindedness, Grit reflects, there is already something of death. She barks at him, tries to fend off his attendance, to arouse him from his doped to-ing and fro-ing by means of attacks and with force, to shake him awake to himself again. 'It can't go on like this. I have no desire to watch you slowly rotting away. Do something, father! Just do something or other. . . . Don't sit round here. Why don't you go back to Zachler at last? Here all you do is sit round and scare off my friends. It can't go on like this. Have you got that?'

In vain. Her father won't be stirred or startled. He gazes with stupid astonishment past Grit and murmurs: 'Plan F . . . Plan F . . .' 'What's that supposed to mean— "plan F"?' Grit

[131]

demands, irritated, but she gets no reply. Her father is silent most of the time. Nonetheless he wants to be near her continually. He has lost all reserve concerning the forward part of the flat. It is no use shouting at him, threatening him or shedding tears of desperation. He follows the trail he must go, blindly without will, unswervingly. Only locked doors and at times blows to the shoulder can stop this body that pushes ahead everywhere, thin though it is.

In the evening he comes to watch television and sits silently on the couch beside Grit. There he remains sunken in himself throughout the programme, only occasionally raises his head in wonder, in response to which stimuli or summons it is impossible to say.

And if she puts up with his presence during these periods— distracted by television films and even, if something appealing is on, all at once and unawares made to feel milder and friendlier towards him again by the illusions of a lovelier world—yet, on the other hand, the occasions when the old man causes her to feel disgusted or turn pale are growing more numerous. Recently it has already happened several times that she has come home in the evening and entered a bathroom which stinks evilly because her father has forgotten to flush his dirt away. That he is letting himself go more and more, indeed is turning into some base creature, does not merely arouse her abhorrence; far more it dismays her that this carefully kept stench is in some way directed at her, or against her, some cryptic message, a signal that seems to have animal origins, which this man who has fallen silent is sending her from a terrible distance. For everything that he gets up to in his idle brooding seems to be done for her sake alone and does in fact seem to want to communicate with her. Next to her on the couch, bent forward over his own stomach and his open fly, he considers the forsakenness, the brown shrivelled fold of skin of his sex, pulls it out, and, having ascertained that Grit is half in the grip of a television programme (but indeed only half), he begins hastily to rub himself, with a haste that hardly any other hand movement of his possesses. Without intending it, Grit,

[132]

to admonish him, has recourse to a wholly alien tone and manner and is transformed into a strict mama: 'For heaven's sake: stop that. For such things we have a toilet, father.'

As he does not obey she knocks his hands out of his lap and tugs his trousers to. Her father gruffly turns his head to one side, folds his arms firmly across his chest, and adopts the nonsensical pose of the master affronted in his own house.

Now Grit becomes aware that a sense of duty and patience can no longer enable her to endure this life together with her father, which has become tangled with dark cunning. Everything is getting worse day by day. More and more frequently she catches herself nowadays in impulses and transformations of her personality that are not remotely welcome and ill become her youth, ruin her own basic levity and joy in living. The way she has to behave at home she often feels as if, at only just past twenty, she were not the daughter of this man but rather the mama, already turned rather odd and elderly, of a senile child. Steadfastly admonishing, threatening, refusing, feeling disturbed and bothered, makes you a loveless, unhappy mother, whether you want it or not, and without Nature having intended it. It makes you pusillanimous and in the long run creates idiosyncrasies and sensitivities that can no longer be got rid of. More powerfully than ever before she becomes aware that only her father is near her and nobody else, not Joseph, no one. It is not without reason that she overdoes the zeal with which she keeps an eye on everything her father gets up to and misses no opportunity to curb him. Sometimes she even accuses herself of 'over-reacting'. But for this very thing there must be a hidden reason.

At all events she feels cornered by the old man dismally slouching around the flat, and imprisoned in a hot, stuffy nest which every passing day makes more twigged-up and impenetrable. Gradually she becomes unfree in her whole body, and at home moves about gloomily and dragging, aware as it were of being the object and prey of the oppressive return home of this man, who did not come to her to rally for a brief spell after a failed professional endeavour (the endeavour,

[133]

that is, to stay on in Oldenburg) but probably even had to fail in Oldenburg *because* he wanted to come to her at all costs and as early as possible. Who now makes no preparations at all to separate from her again, to pull himself together and go outside, or indeed still to recognize an Outside at all. Whose whole staying and seduction was aimed at dragging her, his child, down into his silent hollow and into old age, this false old age of the perpetual idiot, first in an underhand, mental way, then by helping and caring for her, afterwards, however, with ever more shameless means, and in the end with a total, obscene decrepitude. Without having the proper concepts for it, the ultimate meaning of this slow, unremitting clasp becomes suddenly clear to her in a transport of horror: 'But that isn't love!' she cries out, 'that really isn't love!'

Shortly after, one Sunday morning, as she is just imagining how yet again one free day will joylessly slip by under the baneful influence of her lurking, dozing father, she suddenly—after a short panicky pile-up of all her binding instincts—breaks out in a true frenzy of the rage for liberation. Without any preparation she runs to the back and charges into her father's closet, pulls his things out of all the drawers, drags along a big suitcase from the hall and tosses the articles higgledy-piggledy into it. 'You'll only take the essentials from me!' she commands, possessed and raving as she grabs, and racing about in such a way that the packing soom resembles the stripping of meat from some wild animal that has been killed. 'Whatever else you need you can fetch from your Oldenburg flat.'

Her father, who was lying clothed on the bed staring at the ceiling, now stands up without further ado and quietly fetches from the cupboard his shoes, which are in an old bag as he has not gone out for a long time and has always gone about in stockinged feet in the rooms. He puts his shoes on, then goes into the bathroom and combs his hair. He seems to accept without objection, indeed with indifference and acquiescence, that he is to be thrown out headlong. When he comes out of the bathroom he drops the comb from chest-height into the carelessly packed suitcase.

'Come on!' says Grit, red-faced, 'now you're going.'

Her father looks at her with a tender gaze, which suddenly, however, becomes implacable. All he says is: 'As you like.'

Then they drive to the Fehmarn Hotel, where Bekker lived before he met his daughter again and where he also lived as long as she was in hospital. Once again he is given a room facing on to the street, once again on the fourth floor of the narrow new building. Grit accompanies her father to his room. He enters without looking round at all as anyone would do in order to take in the character of a strange room where he will be staying for an indefinite length of time. Instead he goes straight over to the wash-basin, tests the cold and hot running water, and also tests the window fixture with which the curtains and net curtains are moved. Last, he empties an ashtray the chambermaid forgot into the waste-paper basket. Then he sits down on the edge of the narrow bed and folds his hands between his spread legs. 'This is how he will always sit here,' thinks Grit, and of a sudden she is overcome by a fit of repentance and pity. She would already like to take everything back now, and take her father home with her right away. She cries, her eyes clear. 'We'll do it like this for the moment,' she declares, rather more resolutely than she feels, 'and then we'll see how we go on.'

Her father nods; he glances down at the tattered flowery pattern of the bedside runner. All at once Grit kneels beside him and holds his head to her neck. Then she runs out of the room. Immediately her father stands up and begins to unpack his case, arranging the articles of clothing and hanging them up or laying them out with precision in the wardrobe.

On the drive home Grit repeatedly attempts to console herself with the thought that it will undoubtedly do her father good now to be thrown totally on his own resources for once. He was only able to let himself go for so long, she tells herself, because there was always someone there, she herself, that it was worthwhile putting on a miserable show for. Now that is over and he will pull himself together of his own accord, he

[135]

will, God knows, regain his full manhood, he'll work at the reconstruction of his spirit, to return in the end to the Institute after all, and quite certainly not to the worst of positions. On the other hand she does not underestimate the fact that on his own he is more intensely in danger of collapsing once and for all, disappearing without trace among false friends, dust, restlessness and delirium. But conversely, she argues, an instinct for self-preservation must in the end protect him from the very worst. . . . But what kind of lamentable instinct *is* it that is forever stumbling and bucking and that you have to kick and shove like a lame donkey?

But still she imagines that it will end well. The more violently she is oppressed by sorrow and feelings of guilt, the more soberly and self-righteously she attains the conviction that she has acted cruelly, it's true, but for the best and in his interests.

At home she gives a good airing to the closet behind the bathroom where her father dwelt beneath the narrow window, and pushes the few pieces of furniture together in one corner.

That same night she gets the first of a series of phone calls that are to bother and frighten her time and again in the course of the next few weeks. Nothing else can be heard in the receiver but the heavy, lecherous, forest-deep breathing of a man who must have the chest of a giant.